Non Profit Fundraising

How to Engage Influencers for Purpose

(A Practical Guide to Telling Stories That Raise Money)

Norman Blazer

Published By **John Kembrey**

Norman Blazer

All Rights Reserved

Non Profit Fundraising: How to Engage Influencers for Purpose (A Practical Guide to Telling Stories That Raise Money)

ISBN   978-0-9938088-9-0

No part of this guidebook shall be reproduced in any form without permission in writing from the publisher except in the case of brief quotations embodied in critical articles or reviews.

Legal & Disclaimer

The information contained in this book is not designed to replace or take the place of any form of medicine or professional medical advice. The information in this book has been provided for educational & entertainment purposes only.

The information contained in this book has been compiled from sources deemed reliable, and it is accurate to the best of the Author's knowledge; however, the Author cannot guarantee its accuracy and validity and cannot be held liable for any errors or omissions. Changes are periodically made to this book. You must consult your doctor or get professional medical advice before using any of the suggested remedies, techniques, or information in this book.

Upon using the information contained in this book, you agree to hold harmless the Author from and against any damages, costs, and expenses, including any legal fees potentially resulting from the application of any of the information provided by this guide. This disclaimer applies to any damages or injury caused by the use and application, whether directly or indirectly, of any advice or information presented, whether for breach of contract, tort, negligence, personal injury, criminal intent, or under any other cause of action.

You agree to accept all risks of using the information presented inside this book. You need to consult a professional medical practitioner in order to ensure you are both able and healthy enough to participate in this program.

Table Of Contents

Chapter 1: The Purpose Of Nonprofit Organizations 1

Chapter 2: Deciding On A Nonprofit Or For Profit 13

Chapter 3: For Profit Organizations Can Be Altruistic 26

Chapter 4: A Roadmap For Success 35

Chapter 5: How To Use The Dashboard . 46

Chapter 6: What's The Procedure To Obtain Tax-Exempt Status Through The Irs? 64

Chapter 7: Management 72

Chapter 8: Leadership 98

Chapter 9: The Board Of Directors 115

Chapter 10: Compare A Non-Profit Charity To A For-Profit Business 121

Chapter 11: History And Types Of Non-Profits 131

Chapter 12: Board Of Directors 142

Chapter 13: Non-Profit Plan With 21st Century Deliverables - Greens! 151

Chapter 14: What Is A Nonprofit? 162

Chapter 15: Research 165

Chapter 16: Fundraising 175

Chapter 1: The Purpose Of Nonprofit Organizations

Non-profits have been given a specific job in society. Government has set the criteria for these organizations, and consequently, the public expects the role of a nonprofit organization to be. The law has been enacted to clearly define the definition of a non-profit organization as well as the types of tasks they are permitted and not allowed to carry out, and as a result of the nature of products and services they provide, what kind of rewards it can be given for providing those services.

An Nonprofit Organization (NPO), often referred to a non-commercial or not-for-profit organisation, commonly referred to as an NCO (also known as an non-governmental organisation (NGO) It is an entity that makes use of the surplus revenue generated to accomplish their goals, not distributing these as dividends, profits or profits.

The designation of a non-profit organization is not a sign that the organization is not planning to generate a profit however, it does mean that the company does not have owners and the money earned through the operations of the company are not used to benefit owners. The amount that an NPO is able to generate revenue can be limited or the use of these surplus funds could be limited. Although nonprofits are allowed to make surplus profits but they are required to keep them by the organisation to safeguard its own self-interest growth, expansion or other goals.

A non-profit organization is any or voluntary group of citizens with a structure at an individual and national, or even international level. They are governed by people that share the same interests they perform a wide range of humanitarian and service functions and bring the concerns of citizens to the attention of governments, promote and oversee policies, and promote the participation of citizens in politics through dissemination of details. Many are based around specific areas, including the environment, human rights or health. They offer analysis and advice and serve as early warning systems and aid in to monitor and enforce international conventions. Their relationships with the organizations and offices within the United Nations system differs depending upon their mission, location and the mission of an organization.

No matter what name you decide to make use of, the organisation is charged with performing the following services in society, whether as a supplier of services as a watchdog or an expert in the field.

The Purpose

Imagine a puzzle, including all the pieces that are missing in a single image. It's how society operates. Each sector is assigned a duty, role and obligations. If every single sector is doing what is expected, the society can function efficiently.

Here's an description of the different sectors that is accountable for:

The government is accountable for developing infrastructure, leading in the direction of managing and funding the government-sponsored programs. It is however lacking the personnel to run the day-today activities. Most government agencies award grants to charities, holding them accountable for achieving their grant objectives. In this way, the governments oversee the work of the non-profit.

Consider government-funded programs such as Food Stamps, Section 8 as well as Social Security. It is not the government that administers these programs, however they finance them. Public agencies responsible for administering these programs submit their quarterly or monthlyand annual outcomes to the state, local and federal governments, who report the total results (e.g. 80 percent of seniors are on social security . . . (or, Employment Development Department statistics revealed a 9 percent increase in the rate of unemployment). CBOs are also a part of the community. Based Organizations (CBOs) also get funding from government agencies. Being experts in their field CBOs can be a great choice to fill a need that government agencies lack enough resources or the expertise required to solve. CBOs submit monthly reports to the federal government regarding their services and programs as part of the grant (e.g. twenty homeless veterans received construction-related training, ten homeless veterans were allocated positions of entry-level; twenty-five homeless veterans were enrolled in homes that were transitional). The statistics then are analyzed by the organization that administers the award.

A Note About 'Free Money'

A lot of people describe grants as "free money'. Though grant money is not an actual loan and is not required to be returned however, it's not the case, and is frequently mistakenly called. A person who is trying to convince the potential buyer to buy the product or service utilizes this term. This is an attempt to trick unknowing leaders of nonprofit organizations to believe that grant money are a right. The reality is that it's not. Nonprofits are not automatically eligible to receive grants since they are 501(c)(3) tax exempt. 501(c)(3) status for tax exemption. (We will go into this detail in the future.) They wish nonprofit officials to believe that funds are given free of charge without obligations or conditions. However, that isn't factual.

The grant money is provided by funders to non-profit organizations to provide services in a specific amount of time. The grant is then targeted at a particular group of people. The nonprofits do not need to return the funds however, grant funds come with many regulations, limitations as well as expectations. If the grant money is not used in accordance with the conditions and conditions could result in the nonprofit being accused of poor management of funds, penalty, fines as well as the possibility of losing their tax exemption status or, even more severe than that, jail. It is a given that nonprofits have to be working to earn the grant funds.

For profit businesses focus on making money, ensuring their investors satisfied, and developing new markets that are specialized and niche.

For-profit companies plan their day-to-day operations around creating goods or providing services that make a profit. Investors and shareholders who they strive to keep their shareholders and investors happy. The leaders plan their strategies to gain as much prestige and wealth as they can in their positions as leaders. However, from this industry is commerce, employment, and due to the fact that they're rich and require to stay current, the latest advances in technology. The current business environment is awash with firms that show their support to human rights through CSR (Corporate Social Responsibility (CSR) programmes typically gain popularity with the public and also points towards their company's rating (i.e., Fortune 500 and so on.). The status allows companies to give financial support to cause that will benefit their image, and also the local community.

If the government is in charge of regulating and corporations are inventing new technology What sector is responsible for the social programmes? The Nonprofits.

Nonprofits are considered to be charitable, specialized, highly socially-driven, and knowledgeable in their field.

The goal of the non-profit organisation is to fill in the gap that has been left by

Government and For Profit. They do what they are not in their ability to perform. Since they're not governed directly by laws or regulations of the government or influenced by the financial benefits or shareholders the nonprofits can be seen as being honest in their actions. The noble causes of charity motivate volunteers to give their time and money in order to achieve organization's goals and objectives since they are aiming to improve society and not earn money.

Here's a scenario that could aid you in understanding. Think of Hurricane Katrina. The government sent in the National Guard to help restore the order of things, FEMA for aiding in the construction of new homes and also passed legislation to aid the poor (extend employment). For-profit corporations came in and demanded that the insurance companies, individuals as well as the government to take down and build the houses, and clear the lakes and rivers full of trash so that they could restore the city. Who will serve the people of New Orleans? Who actually was involved and contributing to the rebuilding of life of people living who lived in New Orleans? It was the charitable organizations. They provided the Red Cross provided shelter, clothing and food. They also received financial contributions from generous citizens around the world and then distributed them to people that were in the most need. Community-based organizations also assisted by finding Gulf residents temporary housing as well as providing help with relocation, as well as job instruction for people who were denied access to jobs as due to the devastating natural catastrophe. Thus, these non-profits were an intermediary between two industries, performing what that the other two did not have the capacity or were not capable of doing.

In light of the services offered and also the fact that money are returned to the community, organizations that are that are approved by the IRS have a tax-exempt status which allows their donors to enjoy tax advantages. In its wisdom, realized that it would not be able to provide funds for the entirety of nonprofits, however understanding their importance, they created tax incentives for businesses and individuals to help motivate them to donate to nonprofits. The IRS accepts tax write-offs to givers for donations.

Understanding the goals of nonprofit organisations is essential to their successful operation. The IRS makes nonprofit leaders accountable for the rules and regulations that are enacted to regulate them, while the rest of the society is able to expect the kind of services and programs must be offered.

Nonprofits who fail to conform to these regulations can be penalized with fines as well as removal of their tax-exempt status. In the event of a violation non-profit leaders could also face being sentenced to jail. Tax exemption is a privilege that has clear guidelines. The misuse or mismanagement of tax exemption is a matter that can result in severe fines.

Chapter 2: Deciding On A Nonprofit Or For Profit

Some people find that deciding to establish a non-profit organization or for-profit business is an issue. In some cases, misinformation may cause entrepreneurs to choose one route in preference to the other.

It is essential to explore every aspect of any business idea, and starting with a non-profit organization isn't an exception. Establishing a nonprofit organisation that is sustainable and be a significant part of the local community takes a lot of effort. A well-informed and confident choice on whether or not you should start an organization can be achieved if you know the options available to you.

There are a variety of reasons for people to start a non-profit. People have been lied to about "facts" about nonprofit organizations and then begin the process of establishing organizations with the intention of creating something fresh and meaningful that won't need a lot of effort or energy . . . In the end, the guy appearing on his TV Infomercial guarantees it, or else you'll get the refund! Right?

Below are four of the most frequently misunderstood motives for starting Non-profit organisations:

A 501(c)(3)-tax status gives your company free funds. A nonprofit is automatically eligible for grants which you do not require to repay. '

* Non-profits can fund its existence solely through donations and fundraising. You just need to get grants to cover all the expenses.'

• Start a nonprofit and be paid. If you are the founder of an organization that is nonprofit and you are able to earn yourself the salary.'

The process of starting a non-profit is straightforward. You just need to file your papers and get three members to join the board and then get an award - all you need to do is have the grant writer put his name into the grant, and then get reimbursed on the backend. "Just find a grant-writing professional to fill out the grant. This way, you won't need to think about the cost upfront as well as it will motivate the grant writer to perform a top job.'

A business model based upon misinformation is most common reason why nonprofits do not succeed. The founders of nonprofits believe that after they have obtained tax exempt status, grant funds will begin to flow into. However, grants are extremely and competitive. Nonprofits with a long history have a hard to secure regular and constant grant money. The new nonprofits face even greater difficulties. Even though new nonprofits can qualify for funding from seed (start with a $500-$

$25,000) They will have to put a number of basic elements that are in their place. They will discuss these in the future in the Nonprofit Sequencing. These are the components the majority of new nonprofits do not have since they weren't aware they were sought-after by funders. They are also highly extremely competitive and can be tiny amounts. Thus, uninformed entrepreneurs who fail to get these grants in the manner they were promised, end up spending the majority of their time and money to ensure that their businesses are able to survive.

The third reason that nonprofits are ineffective is that the people who run them lack the experience required to effectively run their organisation. From finance to infrastructure and board responsibility to cultivation of donors and the development of collaboration. The truth is that the final decision on how to launch and run a profitable nonprofit must be based on knowing precisely what it takes to run a successful nonprofit. Passion for the cause is great however, there's no replacement for the fundamental understanding of management.

A multitude of businesses apply for IRS tax exemptions each year. Do our communities suffer from numerous issues that merit the influx of applications?

There is no way to say 'no'. Another fact is that there are a number of enthusiastic, dedicated, and concerned people who wish to contribute positively to the world. The majority of nonprofit organizations were founded as a result of the personal trauma, experience or loss. In the case of Susan G. Komen foundation as well as many others were founded by a person who loved them and wanted to make a positive impact and reduce the chance that someone else would suffer the same kind of suffering. In the end, the motives behind creating a nonprofit are worthy of praise. The question is, are you actually required to create another one?

Running a non-profit organization is just similar to operating as a profit-making company however, the income generated by the running of a nonprofit will require more work to bring money in the doors. Nonprofits require strategic planning effective leadership and management including financial management, recruiting, development and training as well as networking, marketing monitoring compliance, evaluation as well as operational expansion and sustainability. The running of a non-profit organization takes lots of effort and time.

A few founders have launched their companies from a point of inspiration, and then failed to carry out proper diligence and conduct research.

The community needs to conduct a survey of its community

* Organisations that provide similar services, the same as competitors.

* The commercial aspects of running an enterprise - establishing the infrastructure

If research was conducted prospective founders could discover that there exist at most five to 10 other companies offering exactly the same or similar the services that their company is expected to provide. However, in the majority of cases this information isn't really relevant due to the fact that a majority of people who establish foundations for non-profit organizations do it due to the desire to be the ones in charge. They also believe that their current competitors are offering the services as they ought to be done, or missing an important component.

Instead of working with organisations already offering the services by way of volunteer as a board member, a volunteer or paid staff, and bridging the gap between internal and external service the community, individuals continue to add an increasing number of organizations on be added to the roster of non-profit organizations.

An excellent test to use that community leaders with passion should determine which route to choose is:

Are you prone to falling asleep in your bed thinking about the impact that your company will have on the local neighborhood?

Are you awakened by innovative and novel strategies for funding your company?

Are you connected to companies and people who can assist in advancing your mission?

If you can answer these questions is 'yes' investigate the local community, its requirements along with competitors and the sources available to support the nonprofit and continue to grow. If you answer "usually is the answer, or no' think about the options for starting an organization that is non-profit.

* Become a volunteer. Volunteers can create a massive impact for the life of an organisation. Many times, volunteers exhibit dedication and enthusiasm and get asked to fill crucial roles within the organisation. In some cases, they are as a valuable resource they're appointed as a employee.

Join the board. Board members act as the strategic arm of the company. They have the responsibility of guiding the company through leadership knowledge, and financial assistance. Being a member of the board, you can provide suggestions for closing any gaps in service and help strengthen the operation of the organisation within the local neighborhood.

Apply to become a staff member. Find a job that is important within the company. Change is best made inside. If you're a staff member paid, you'll be able to contribute towards the delivery of high-quality services, providing important feedback and insights in addition to the benefit of working in an organisation that is in perfect alignment with your goals and passions.

The process of starting a non-profit organization requires an enormous amount of work. Making it operational is not an easy job also. It is also a challenge to sustain the organization. Once a person has the right infrastructure, the company can turn into a useful asset for communities. It is essential that a lot of studies are conducted before starting a huge project. Some times, the results help to strengthen the founding team's motivation to establish the company. Sometimes, they help give a more realistic view on satisfying the requirements of people in the community as opposed to.

fulfilling a specific need or the options available to meet that need.

Participating in volunteer activities, such as becoming a director or a paid employee for an organization that provides similar services can be an ideal way of getting an experience that is hands-on. The ability to gain experience is crucial for getting over the obstacles and bumps that come with being an entrepreneur. It's a good idea to perform your test runs in a setting in which everything is unaffected by the decisions you make. Think about volunteering for another group particularly if this is your first time in the non-profit sector. It is a great way to gain knowledge as well as meet prospective staff members and directors for your group but most important, experience the many aspects you need to know about running your organization before jumping into the water.

Non-profit organizations are able to (and must) earn profits.

The operating costs of nonprofits are as do for-profit businesses. The most successful nonprofit organizations should have a broad sources of funds to fund the overhead expenses (not normally paid for through grants) and programs & services, in addition to the costs of building capacity. The diversified stream of funding should consist of unrestricted money and line items allocated (restricted) which must be covered through contributions, grants, fees/dues or gifts, fundraisers such as fee for service or in-kind contributions, match-funds, sponsorships and other donations. As per IRS guidelines and rules, any revenue earned by nonprofits are required to be returned to the local community.

Profits don't just occur. It takes a strategies. The development and implementation of this strategy falls under the control of the Board of Directors. Further details will be provided further on the roles and duties of Board members. However, it is vital to are able to count on an active and knowledgeable board to help you raise the money needed to support the nonprofit you run.

As the founder, you'll be required to decide on the role you'll assume in the direction. Are you the Executive Director? This is a position that's paid with the responsibility of implementing the objectives of the organisation. Will you serve as the president? This position is accountable to guide the direction of the company but is not a salary-based job. Further information about this in the book 'The Nonprofit Board of Directors What to do to create an Eco-friendly Nonprofit organization' eBook. It is a crucial choice.

Chapter 3: For Profit Organizations Can Be Altruistic

For profit organizations can become effective philanthropic stakeholders in the community through its grant making and Corporate Social Responsibility (CSR) programs. For profits typically give up to 5% of its gross revenue to nonprofit organizations that help further its philanthropic giving initiatives. However, it is not a legal requirement that revenue generated by the company must be reinvested back into the community. For profit companies can amass as much revenue for its investors, owners, and company without restriction or limitation. Concerns tend to focus more on how executive leaders handle investments, stocks and capital gains tax issues.

The decision to incorporate a company as a nonprofit or for profit comes down to the type of impact a founder wants to make in his or her community. For those who want to focus on making a social impact, influencing legislation and public policy, and creating/enforcing ethical standards, then starting a nonprofit is the most logical path. For those wanting to generate revenue by creating new products or services, starting a for-profit is the most logical path.

If your heart is with making a difference that will bring about social change, start a nonprofit. If your heart is with making a difference that will impact an industry or business sector, start a for-profit. But know that starting a business requires a lot of hard work and dedication. Both entities will require the same amount of planning, strategizing, and marketing efforts. There is no "easier" route.

Consider having an in depth conversation with several leaders from both sectors to find out all that it takes to incorporate and run a successful business. Nothing beats first hand knowledge, and no one knows the business better than the leader tasked to take the company to the next level year after year. Once you've had several conversations, completed research on the focus of your organization, and assessed your community needs, the decision should be clear as to which path is best for what you're trying to accomplish.

A Self-Guided Checklist of Questions

Upon completion of this survey of questions you should have a better idea of whether you should start a nonprofit or for profit organization.

Benchmark Question

Is Your Answer

Best Suited Organization

Am I passionate about a cause?

x Yes

p No

x Nonprofit

x For Profit

Is the org meeting an unmet need?

x Yes

p No

x Nonprofit

x For Profit

Is there another org that provides the same service?

x Yes

p No

x Nonprofit

x For Profit

Is my service/ product uniquely different?

x Yes

p No

x Nonprofit

x For Profit

Have I received tax exempt status from the IRS - 501(c)(3)?

x Yes

p No

x Nonprofit

o For Profit

Does my service/product qualify For philanthropic funding?

x Yes

p No

x Nonprofit

o For Profit

Do I have an experienced Board?

x Yes

p No

x Nonprofit

o For Profit

Am I looking to make a large profit

x Yes

p No

x Nonprofit

x For Profit

Is my budget cycle designed to reinvest all funds back into the community?

x Yes

p No

x Nonprofit

o For Profit

Do I have investors to repay?

x Yes

p No

o Nonprofit

x For Profit

Do I have systems in place to support fundraising goals?

x Yes

p No

x Nonprofit

o For Profit

Will my organization seek grant funding?

x Yes

p No

x Nonprofit

o For Profit

Have I identified at least 3 streams of revenue?

x Yes

p No

x Nonprofit

o For Profit

Is my primary function to improve a social issue?

x Yes

p No

x Nonprofit

o For Profit

If you answered more than 8 of these questions "NO" then you probably should not start a nonprofit organization. Speak to a professional business manager about starting a for profit business

The Dashboard and Nonprofit Sequencing

Starting a nonprofit organization is neither as simple nor as difficult as people may think. But it does take hours of work to 'start' a nonprofit. There is a process that founders must follow in order to start a nonprofit organization.

Chapter 4: A Roadmap For Success

Often, founders put the cart before the horse in terms of starting a nonprofit organization. While well intentioned, founders sometimes jump to the middle of the development process, by passing crucial elements that are paramount to the organization's success.

There are recommended steps in starting a successful nonprofit organization. I provide a step-by-step template on how to complete each of these elements in my eBook "Developing the Nonprofit Infrastructure". But for the purpose of this conversation, it's called Nonprofit Sequencing. Nonprofit sequencing offers founders a roadmap for developing a nonprofit organization in the most effective manner.

Nonprofit Sequencing is a tool for developing a strong, solid, and sustainable nonprofit organization. Nonprofit sequencing is a term used to describe the process for developing a successful nonprofit organization. Sequencing speaks to the order in which specific elements of the organization should be developed.

Nonprofit sequencing helps the community leader understand the purpose and function of a nonprofit organization and what needs to be in place prior to receiving funding. Emphasis is placed on 'eligibility for receiving funding' because this is the number one concern listed by community leaders in community assessments, focus groups, surveys and round tables. Emphasis is also placed on funding because "if organizations are not able to keep their doors open to provide services to the community or pay staff to deliver programs and services, then everything else becomes irrelevant".

A strong organization is one that makes a long-term impact in the community. Long term suggests the ability to run the organization in such a way that it becomes the mainstay of the community.

One very useful tool in the development of a successful nonprofit organization is a document called the Dashboard. A dashboard on a vehicle provides the owner with valuable information about the condition of the vehicle. Similarly, a dashboard for a nonprofit will do the same.

- How much fuel is in the tank? Speaks to organizational finances

- What speed the car is going? What is the rate of growth of the organization

- RPMS, the car's horsepower? The organization's ability to draw supporters, or influence change in the community

- Navigation System – Strategy, forecasting (future)

- Engine/Oil/Brakes – Indicates the stability of the organization's infrastructure

- No brakes – A collision waiting to happen

- No oil - blocked engine; no movement

The dashboard is a great tool for the entire organization. It is an at-a-glance look at the most important elements of the organization. It visually illustrates the pulse of the inner and outer workings of the business.

It is a perfect tool for creating a solid nonprofit organization. For organizations just starting out, it serves as a guide in creating a fully fundable organization. For organizations in the midst of development or even seasoned organizations with a long history, the dashboard can help community leaders get their organizations on course, and stay the course powerfully.

Nonprofit Sequencing – The Dashboard

Roadmap for Success

1

ORGANIZATION CONCEPT ORGANIZATION

2

INFRASTRUCTURE

3

ORGANIZATION DEVELOPMENT

4

OPERATION INFRASTRUCTURE

5

OPERATION SUSTAINABILITY

Mission Statement

Staff Roles &

Experience

Articles of Incorporation

Forms/Documents Templates

Fund

 Development

- Philosophy
- Job Descriptions
- Staff
- By-Laws
- Tracking/Reporting Systems
- Board Contribution
- Give/Get/Dues
- Purpose
- Orientation Training
- Staff/Board
- Board Selection
- Materials &
- Supplies
- Program Generated Revenue
- Fee for Service
- Organization History

Position Description

Board of Directors

501(C)(3)

Tax Exemption

Equipment

Grants, Gifts, Sponsors

Target Audience Demographics

Job Description Ancillary Consultants

Board Training

Technology (Software/Hardware)

Fundraising Events & Activities

Program Description

Services/Product

Board of Directors

Manual

Fiver Year Strategic Plan

Website

Collaborations

Goals & Objectives

Employee Manual

Staff Hiring

GuideStar/

Dunn&Bradstreet

In-Kind Contributions

Measurable Outcomes

Volunteer Manual

Staff Training

Social Media

Capital/Endowment Campaign

Annual Budget

Intern Manual

ng

Vunteer

Volunteer Training

Branded Products

Planned Gifts

Starting

The basic elements needed to start a nonprofit organization

Structuring

Elements needed to run the nonprofit like a for profit business

Programs & Services that make an impact in your community

Infrastructure design elements that ensure longevity

Sustaining

Operation practices that increases the sustainability of a nonprofit organization

Diversifying your funding stream to ensure the longevity of the organization

The Dashboard is an organization's roadmap for success. Use this tool as a resource to help support the organization, just like the dashboard is used for vehicles.

The more completed items an organization has in each column moving to the right, the higher ranked the organization would be with a Funder. The goal is to have all of these items in place.

Is that reality? Maybe not right away. But that is the goal! For with each of these items, not only does the organization's value in terms of funding increase, but value in terms of the organization running more effectively and efficiently. With more of these items in place, it's safe to say the more tools and resources community leaders have to help them become more successful.

Most organizations start at Column 3. Someone decides to start a nonprofit, so they file the papers and figure out the foundational stuff (Columns 1 and 2) later, when it's required, usually for a grant. This is typical, and causes a lot of backtracking to get all of the elements in place. But it usually gets figured out.

The Dashboard has been designed to help community leaders understand the process and complete each section in order. The goal is to have all of these elements in place as soon as possible – and definitely before you approach a grant writer or a funder.

Rows 4 & 5 reflect advanced organizations, and are where every nonprofit should strive to be, as they have all the elements of a strong and successful nonprofit organization.

Chapter 5: How To Use The Dashboard

The Dashboard is to be used as a living tool. Meaning, it should be reviewed at every staff meeting: weekly, monthly, etc. Ideally the Executive Director, along with Administrators (Program Directors, Program Managers, Accountant, etc.) will design the Dashboard. But every staff member should be provided with a copy and regular updates.

In order for it to be used At-A-Glance as intended, there is a color chart and legend assigned to help give leaders a quick view of what's going on. A RED box would indicate that this issue is either not being addressed or a poor job has been done on accomplishing the goals associated with the issue. A GREEN box would indicate that this issue has been successfully accomplished or is doing well. A YELLOW box would indicate that this issue has been handled at a mediocre level and could use improvement, or needs to be considered next as an item of importance. If the box is left WHITE, it means that it is an element that needs to be considered in the future, and is on the dashboard because it is important (e.g., registration). For simplicity, these are the only colors to be used on the Dashboard. Leaders can quickly look at the document and have meaningful conversations regarding the issues that need to be addressed given the color of each issue and the goal of the meeting. Some of the best meetings will come from simply reviewing the dashboard. Provide each attendee with three crayons (Red, Green, Yellow and White) and go through the document, assigning the appropriate colors. There is a book, much later in the series that discusses how to effectively use the Dashboard for effective meetings. The Dashboard essentially helps the meeting facilitator create a productive meeting by creating a useful agenda, action items, and managing time.

Unlike a 25-page business plan, or a 5-page report, the one page Dashboard is an effective and efficient tool that can assist community leaders with getting and keeping their organizations on point for successful business development.

The Roles and Responsibilities of Nonprofit Leaders

It is important to understand the leadership roles in a nonprofit organization. It becomes extremely important in developing the strategy, programs and services, and funding structure for the agency. Each of these roles impacts the decision-making process of the organization.

The basic structure of a nonprofit encompasses two sides, the visionary team and the implementation team. The visionary team is the Board of Directors, and comprises the leaders who are responsible for the decision-making of the organization. They create the purpose, vision, and overall direction of the nonprofit. They have a fiduciary responsibility to represent the organization, and in doing so, are held legally responsible for all contractual obligations entered into by the organization. Because the board is responsible for things like growth and expansion, ensuring the solubility of the organization, and hiring a qualified leader to manage the day-to day operations, they are not involved with the actual implementation side of the organization. They hire and work closely with an Executive Director who is responsible for implementation.

Ideally, the Board of Directors work in partnership with the Executive Director who apprises them of the progress and challenges going on in the daily operation of the organization. The President leads the Board of Directors, and ultimately has the most power in the nonprofit organization. This is especially important to know when starting a nonprofit. There have been countless instances when a founder starts an organization, builds the board, staff, and agency from the ground up, and is fired by the board. Legally, this can happen. In the legal structure of a nonprofit organization the Executive Director reports to the Board of Directors. It is one of the Board's fiduciary responsibilities to hire and/or fire the Executive Director.

The implementation team, lead by the Executive Director, is responsible for carrying out the vision of the organization. A paid staff is responsible for delivering programs and services to the community. The staff members, including consultants, report to the Executive Director. The Executive Director in turn keeps the Board of Directors abreast of program, fiscal, staffing, volunteer, community, collaborative and political successes and challenges that may impact the daily operations during monthly Board of Directors' meetings. The diagram depicts the structure of an ideal nonprofit organization

Decision-Making Body Implementation Body

President

Vice-President

Executive Director

Treasurer

Administrative Assistant

Secretary

Program Director

Board Members

Program

Manager

Volunteers

Consultants

Program Coordinator

Program Coordinator

Program Coordinator

Selecting a Board of Directors

The most important thing to consider when establishing a non-profit is the effort and commitment needed to ensure that the company is sustainable. One of the most crucial options a founder has to take is to choose the board members.

The Board of Directors is the authority that decides the direction of the business. It is responsible for establishing the direction and vision for the business However, most importantly is their responsibility for fundraising funds that will keep the organization viable and long-lasting. of the business.

However, most founders is the one who starts the business with relatives and friends as officials. It's not a problem but, usually, relatives and friends accept the position as they believe in the founder. They're just not qualified to manage the business or to raise funds. This could be a huge disadvantage when it comes to the beginning and expanding an organization.

The recruitment of Board members who are experienced and/or experts with the talents, capabilities, dedication and the resources required to help support the organization's expansion is essential to the overall success of a charity.

It's one thing to be a founder and work for a long time in the role of the founder. However, it's quite another to have a single person responsible for the everyday operations, expansion and long-term sustainability of an enterprise. In the absence of a group that is able to be able to tackle the task with aplomb is an enormous mistake in making sure that you can achieve your vision as a chief executive.

Two crucial points to consider when selecting members of the Board of Directors:

1. Make sure you know who is joining your board. There are many people who join boards due to various motives. Politics and personal agendas influence the outcome of the choices made by board members. The decisions made by the board can have a significant impact on the direction taken by the company.

Who is the authority? In the sector of nonprofits is The Board of Directors. The person with the most power for a nonprofit is the Board president, and not the Executive Director. According to law, the Board can hire and remove executive directors. regardless of whether they are the director who founded the organization. That's why selecting the board and the training process is vital.

Implementing a selection procedure for board members helps determine the commitment level of an individual to the organization's goals, mission, and knowledge. Conducting a board-training and development plan can make sure that decisions made by the board align with the business's mission and goals. Implementation and establishment of methods and procedures could significantly affect the results of Board the decisions.

2. The Board of Directors has an obligation of fiduciary towards the company. They should be picked not only based on their abilities to serve as visionaries, fundraisers and the leaders of the organization, but also because of their capacity to take tough choices. The Board is accountable to the law for their decisions in behalf of the institution. This is the reason Directors & Officers insurance is mandatory to protect the Board. It is possible to be legally liable. It is important to have board members who

are able to withstand the scrutiny, stand up to the pressure and take professionally-minded decisions for the benefit of their organization and with the highest interest of the business.

The selection of an Board is an additional factor in submitting funding proposals. Funders will look at Board of Directors and their affiliations while deciding which organisations to support. The board's quality aids funders in getting a sense about the sustainability of the company. The kind of people who run the company defines strong boards. When choosing board members you must take into consideration the crucial role they play in the sustainability and growth of the business.

The Executive Director's role within a non-profit organization

The job description of the Executive Director job at an organization can cause an anxiety and dismay in some people. The job description lists everything from strategic planning to fundraising, daily operations creating and training staff and community outreach to networking, both written and oral communications, board training, development, management, accounting and public speaking just to mention a few.

Through the years as well as with the difficult economic conditions Executive Directors are called upon to perform ever more. It is important to ensure for Executive Directors to possess many abilities, it's also crucial that an Executive Director be efficient. Being the head in the implementation side of the business (the Board of Directors functioning as the decision-making and visionary aspect of the business) and the Executive Director's effectiveness is based on the ability of his or her team to maximise resources and assign responsibility.

Working with Board members in creating a strategy for growth and longevity of the business is crucial. This collaboration helps Executive Directors to make choices in the day-to-day activities of the company for example, the hiring of consultants to handle other ancillary tasks like hiring, writing grants and marketing.

The main responsibility of an Executive Director's job is to oversee the business. The most successful leader does amazing job at having their board support the Executive Director in their funding positions so that will be able to handle. The Executive Director often is so absorbed in trying to manage everything that they get trapped in the middle of working on the small details so that high-level management cannot accomplish. A successful Executive Director is one who is able to ensure the progress of the company. i.e. components of the strategy plan he or she worked together with the Board to create are in place, objectives are being achieved as well as partnerships developing to improve the institution's structure and expand its influence.

The day-to-day operational activities, i.e., the success of the implementation of programs and services are under the control for the Director of Executive. Fundraising is the primary driver that drives the daily activities. While the ED has a crucial role in connecting all efforts to raise funds into a coherent and efficient strategic plan it's crucial to understand that this is most effectively accomplished through the ED in charge of the fundraising effort, not. managing it all. The management of the efforts frees the ED to look further ahead to reach objectives that will lead to long-term programmes and services. The pressure of daily routines hinders the ED from accomplishing the task in managing daily activities.

The Legal Formation of A Nonprofit Organization

Starting an IRS-approved non-profit could be a daunting process. It takes a lot of time and effort to finish the required paperwork, particularly when the person who is completing the forms does not have the necessary knowledge or expertise to respond to the inquiries in a manner that is satisfactory to the IRS. The process of obtaining approval to operate as a tax-exempt entity involves more than filling in the forms, it also is a requirement to meet the standards that the United States' Internal Revenue Service is establishing in order for an entity to obtain the tax exemption status.

Who can you choose to establish your non-profit organisation?

There are a variety of options for founders who want to form their own nonprofit entities: lawyers or online firms, as well as consultants. What is the best option for you? It all depends on the budget you have set and how customizable you'd like the legal and corporate documents to be. the corporation. Lawyers generally charge hourly fee to complete documents that can be expensive. But, if the organization is to become an integral element of the foundation that is a legacy of the family (e.g. the foundations for families) there are legal issues that need the specialist expertise of an attorney, and it it is sensible to get an attorney form the company. If the founding members have formed a nonprofit organization based on community or a nonprofit, consulting a professional with an experience of aiding nonprofits to achieve tax exemptions is a good option. Consult with friends. For Executive Directors, or Board members from established non-profits who have filled out their forms. The best method to find professionals who are qualified.

Other options are available however, such as the online businesses. These companies are typically economical and enable owners to sign the documents on the internet. The most important thing to think about is whether the content of your company will be able to read as the standard boilerplate or reflect particular characteristics of the company that make it distinctive. If the company's website provides the possibility of speaking with an agent, perhaps your business will be given the chance to verify that the language you use is unique and reflects your company. Many submission methods just require the completion of the standard form. The information is incorporated into an appropriate template. Keep in mind that the business pays to finish the documents. An entrepreneur should aim to establish their company with a strong foundation. The founder should be looking for more than getting their papers done. An Founder must want their Bylaws and Articles of Incorporation as a representation of the organisation's goal, mission and goals in the sense that they're the official document that communicates these and much more in the eyes of the IRS as well as the public as well as funders.

Nonprofits are created under the authority that is the Internal Revenue Service. The IRS is the government agency with the authority to regulate, approve and, in the event of need, remove nonprofit entities. Standards are in place to determine whether an entity is able to function as an organization that is a nonprofit. It is advised that founders work with professionals to help them complete the paperwork required for the creation procedure.

Chapter 6: What's The Procedure To Obtain Tax-Exempt Status Through The Irs?

These are the steps to follow for legalizing a nonprofit:

1. Choose; verify the availability of NPO name with Secretary of State.

2. Filing Articles of Incorporation in the state in which the business will be operating.

3. The organization's By Laws

4. Send your approved Articles of Incorporation By Laws, and IRS Form 1023 to IRS in order to request that your business be approved to receive Tax Exemption status.

First thing to take is to establish whether your company is able to use its name. Whoever you select to aid you in the legal process of forming your non-profit organization must verify that your company's name with the Secretary State. It is essential to include the name of your nonprofit organization and it should include "Corporation" or "Incorporated" or an abbreviation of these phrases for example "Inc." or "Corp." The majority of states do prohibit two businesses with identical names, nor would they permit your business to use a name which looks identical to the name of another business.

It is then time to establish the goal for the business. This is often stated within the statement of mission. It is one of the most significant decisions that you make when it pertains to the creation of your organization. Make sure you are particular. The reviewers will contact your and inquire regarding your company The goals of the business as well as the frequency with which services will be offered and the place where the services are provided and the length of the program and whether there are charges associated with the services. Be sure to include as much precise information as you can. Additionally, you should provide quantifiable targets, outcomes and goals for every service you provide. I guide you through the process of creating the various statements I discuss within "Developing the Nonprofit Infrastructure," If you've yet to write them, make sure to get this powerful tool. This will spare you a lot of stress and allow you to make the writing portion of the report IRS evaluates to decide whether they will approve the request for tax exempt status simple and straightforward.

However, for the purposes of this guideline then, you must filling out your Articles of incorporation. The process informs the state that you are planning to start a business within the state. If you want to establish an organization that is nonprofit in order to be a nonprofit, you need to file your documents of incorporation (sometimes known as"certificate of incorporation" or "certificate of incorporation" or "charter document" or "articles of organization") with the state, and also be required to pay a filing fee. The fee for filing generally varies between $30 and $125 based upon the state. When filing an Articles of Incorporation essentially forms a company; once accepted, you will be able to operate as a legal person, not in the form of a 501(c)(3) tax-exempt non-profit.

The final process is to write your company's By Laws. Bylaws define the guidelines and regulations that govern how nonprofit organizations can operate and how it will be managed. While there is no standard standards for content in bylaws generally, they establish the internal procedures and rules for nonprofit organizations that address issues such as:

* The responsibilities and existence of corporate officers and directors.

* The number of directors' boards as well as the method and duration of their term

- When and where the board meeting will take place and who will hold the meetings.

- How will the directors' board be able to function?

* How grant funds are distributed (some grantees require that their Bylaws have a prohibition on those who exercise authority to supervise others from benefiting from grant money)

After the documents are completed, the By Statutes as well as Articles of Incorporation together with the details of the company's policies, services and directors of the board must be sent to the IRS to be approved for tax exemption.

When these fundamental elements have been agreed upon, a group of directors is required to be appointed to act as the decision-making institution. Most the board members of a nonprofit organization include family and friends of the founding. This is not recommended as members of the boards are additionally responsible for raising funds in addition to providing guidance and support for the company. Family and friends members although they are supportive, generally don't have the necessary skills to fulfill the obligations of fiduciary responsibility that come with the duties of a director of the board. Foundations, public agencies or funders as well as potential board members generally ask for a list of board members along with any affiliations (profession) to assess the sustainability of your organization. If your board members do not have the experience, knowledge or add value to the company, their importance as leaders within the field the company was created to be a leader in is diminished. It can be the difference between receiving funds or getting it denied, specifically when it comes to newly established nonprofits who don't have a proven experience. It is imperative to have experienced Board members is to your accomplishment. Some adventurous individuals might decide to face the daunting task of filing the documents by themselves. Some may look on the Internet for businesses that offer inexpensive and speedy turnaround options to establish nonprofit organizations. Consultants may also provide the same services but usually with greater costs than companies that are internet-based since they generally offer the most customized service. Web-based firms typically offer generic or canned responses to queries that could set warning signals to IRS examiners, which can lead to delays in approval or even a complete rejection. It is always recommended to seek out referrals from companies which have been successful in obtaining their IRS recognized tax approval.

When this information is accepted and the company is approved, it will be provided an Tax Exemption status. The organization is then granted an Tax Exempt Letter bearing the organization's Tax Identification Number

(TIN), an official date for incorporation, as well an outline of the products, programs and/or services the business can offer pursuant to the exemption.

Based on the details provided (whether or whether it is in line with the requirements) If the IRS is in a state of backlog depending on the workload of the designated caseworker the process of reviewing can take from 6 weeks and 6 months before obtaining the IRS's decision. Some submissions do not get approval.

Chapter 7: Management

In this book, we'll discuss all the aspects involved in managing a non-profit. Let us begin with you!

People often mistakenly associate the terms "leadership" and "management. Both are very different skills. One can be a weak leader, and an excellent leader could be a bad leader. Both roles require trust, vision as well as communication are crucial. As the leader concentrates on the future direction of the company as a business while the manager is focused on the way we can in the direction of getting there.

Management refers to the method of reaching organizational objectives by using and utilizing the assets (human or financial) other) of the business. It is achieved through three methods:

1. Develop the purpose and plan of your company or the region that is responsible.

2. Organize the staff and distribute funds to support this strategy.

3. Train to measure and adapt strategies, resources or methods in order to get the best outcomes.

How do you handle it? Most people don't. They have regular meeting with staff, celebrate birthdays and display inspiring messages hung around in the workplace. There are even documents to fill in and create a number of documents. If told they're not a good manager, individuals are stunned and refer to the many jobs they've been performing.

One of the most important characteristics that a great manager has is how much time shared with the team each individually as well as as collectively. Managers and their workers should talk about the tasks required and the necessary training for the work, ensuring that employees are able to perform the work as well as the evaluation of the task after it has been completed, including praise for the execution of the task and ideas for improvement. This is a huge job.

The Management Team

The typical nonprofit of mid-sized size will include at its helm its executive director (or pastor president, the chief executive officer) and three senior managers. The person who will be directly accountable to the director's executive will likely to be responsible for accounting both expenses and revenue and paying bills as well as preparing all accounting reports and financial reports. Based on the how big the company is and the desired status (in the declining or declining order) The title of the position might be chief financial officers (CFO) or vice president of finance, or the finance manager.

The manager who is second in line may be a vice-president of fundraising, vice for institutional advancement or even a fundraiser. They are the ones who oversee the entire fundraising process and all donor interactions.

The third principal manager of an organization of a medium size is the one who is responsible for providing the services. They can refer as the program director, the director of ministry, director for apostolic works, or anything specifically associated with the particular institution.

The three roles form the team of management that reports to the director of executive. I can't stress enough the necessity that these managers at the top regularly meet and stay coordinated. The meeting should take place even when the executive director can't be in attendance. If they are able to handle operational concerns, then the executive director will be able to concentrate on strategy, mission, and fundraising.

Most nonprofits' head of the organization isn't trained to be a leader in business and, in the absence of guidance of his staff and team, tends to make choices based on his personal experience and not on any prior knowledge. It is especially obvious in religious organizations that have their chief executive as charity is a priest, or a minister who has studied for several years in graduate and college school but, most likely, did not take an accounting or business class. In a recent instance an ordained priest who is the executive director for a significant charity, asked me about was a P&L is.

It is essential that the group, in conjunction as the Executive Director create plans and keep in touch regularly on progress and difficulties. Every member needs a place in the decision-making process when it comes to important issues. The interdependence needs input from three supervisors: finance, fundraising as well as program execution. In particular, even though fundraising does not play a role in the provision of services, they're out in the streets contacting people, and can be the most reliable source to provide information on the opinions of donors and their considering about the company and the things they would like to see supported financially.

Having a Plan

The initial step is to develop a strategy. It doesn't matter if it's a corporate strategy or department's goals There must be an "what we are going to accomplish by when, done by whom," or like we'll talk about in Chapter 7 the GOSPA plan. GOSPA strategy.

Everyone in the workplace should not just comprehend and be aware of this program, but should also be aware of the specific goals that they need to achieve in order in order to perform their job and understand how their work is connected to the success of the company or department. Performance.

The most appropriate tools

Managers who are successful have goals that are clear for their staff members, and aiding them in determining how they can reach those goals and assist in providing guidance in order to develop the necessary skills for achieving those goals.

The most common belief is that employees have the knowledge to perform their job. A lot of times, charity, employees are drawn to the cause for different motives other than the best use of their abilities. The employees do not have expertise nor the training required for the roles that they are assigned. Managers must be aware of the strengths and weaknesses of each employee, and where possible, place the employees to roles in which they will be able to excel right away. However, the majority of companies don't have the possibility. Therefore, it is recommended to invest in training, provide internal training or even mentor the employee, or be prepared for to see subpar quality of work.

It is possible to train in a simple manner. Create a plan of what to do and present the conditions to allow for alternatives or options, and establish an alternate procedure. The measurement of the objective or standard is essential. It can counterbalance emotions that justify "she is so aligned with the mission" or "he is so nice." Management has the responsibility of dealing with substandard conduct.

Regularly scheduled meetings, reviews and building skills

A key skill required by managers is their ability to motivate change. It is a matter of reviewing regularly the work of every employee noting the weaknesses as well as the successes, then providing appropriate strategies for improvement. You should then follow-up with a discussion of how things went as planned and what could have gone wrong and how you can improve. This is an opportunity to gain knowledge.

The measurement can be based on whether an individual completed the work with sufficient quantity. If you are greeted with the positive result it is possible to use phrases like "Wow. What a great thing you did. How did you accomplish that?" If the outcome was not positive, respond with "What occurred that stopped you from meeting this goal?" Identifying the reasons and the place where the process fell down can help employees solve the issue. Managers may need consider other solutions for helping employees achieve the goal.

It's impossible to survive without the help of managers. Indeed, I would say that the role of a manager at the top is one of the most difficult jobs of all jobs in any business. The person in charge has to manage employee concerns but is also expected to not be a victim of all issues from a personal perspective and also have the corporate view. I can remember my very first management position. The issue was the management of employee relations in order to communicate in a manner that was respectful. The boss was frank and said it was not necessary for us to be treated, as management, the same way since we were able to see the purpose of the discussion. Ouch! There's no reason to feel sensitive towards me since I was the manager?

Non-profits must be cautious not to attempt to cut costs by not bringing on managers, or reducing management posts. Managers' role is crucial in helping teams focus on optimal utilization of their resources, however, they also need to recognize the opportunities and challenges that must be dealt with. If you feel that your manager does not contribute value by addressing these issues then you'll need to hire a fresh manager and not simply a job.

Vision and honesty of the individual.

Employers must not only be motivated by their own goals, but they need to have a purpose for the work they do. They are looking for ways to understand what their roles are and how they can add worth. If you are able to make employees aware of their contribution and worth, the more loyal employees will become. In addition, discussing the reasons of your actions assists them in making more informed decisions, make better suggestions, and perform better together. I've never understood management who do not share their the information. In fact, do you really would like them to believe in you but do you have confidence in them?

One of the easiest ways to accomplish this is to make public your team's objectives and goals. Conduct regular meetings about the team's performance, as well as individual and collective achievements. Invite members of your team to give the speeches.

They are grateful for the acknowledgement as it reduces job for the boss!

Remarks on public, private criticism

I had a time when I wanted to have an employee meeting for my sales staff, but my boss pulled me aside and advised me to do it with a different method. He was aware that I was irritated by the poor performance and was planning hit them with a hammer (a very common tactic in the 1980s). He wanted to know what percentages of the people were doing poorly among the ten participants. I replied that it was about four. He replied, "So, you are going to punish six producers because you are mad at the other four?"

I'll never forget it. Even if I'm angry to everyone else and everyone else, an openly criticized behavior creates a negative impression on the mouth of everyone. The effect is that it doesn't inspire anyone to be successful. It is better to bring every nonperformer into the office, and then identify the problem as well as the individual's shortcomings and provide suggestions on how they can improve.

In addition I also know that I am not happy when I'm being judged. Even though it can impact my behavior in the future however, I stand a high likelihood of getting angry at my boss for not being able to comprehend my circumstance. It's better to emphasize the positive aspects about the individual in relation to the job, then discuss the outcomes in comparison to the expectations and then ask the reason why a shortfall was incurred.

Don't don't ever share negative feedback by email. Make sure to discuss issues in person when possible or via phone when there's no feasible means of meeting within a reasonable time. If you must mail an email be sure to rest on it for a while and then verify your message's authenticity and tone after you've calmed down.

Love

The word "love" sounds like a bizarre term in a book about business and even for a non-profit. It's not just about having have lunch with a person. It's about wanting the very highest for them. When I begin a new job I will ask my workers why they're in this position and what they would like to get from the experience. Then, I explain to them that a one of my responsibilities is to assist them in achieving whatever goals they have, whether it's to establish a company and move on to another firm or stay with the company until she is pregnant. If they see some purpose in their work will strive more hard to attain. The downside? You might lose a good employee. However, I believe that the best employees will be loyal to you based on your relationships with them and their relationship the other employees have with you. Golden rule is the ideal approach to living!

It's important to keep in touch with every employee regularly and not only to ask, "How are you doing?" Find out about them, their families and the challenges they face. This isn't to say to make acquaintances with all of them. Also, you're not the camp counselor or bank. However, you must be interested and wish your staff all the most successful.

If your employee feels that you are concerned, the person will certainly accept feedback much more readily and may even be willing to go above and beyond. Also, don't be shocked if the impression isn't reciprocated, or, if not, you do not feel the feeling. You're the boss, not a partner. It's not what you want to be. The goal is to take care of, cherish, your employees.

Hiring

It's awe-inspiring for me that so many businesses do not have an official hiring procedure. It is rare to see during the process of hiring anyone asking more deeply about the particular qualities or abilities that are listed included in the job description. If they are able to look up the skills they are looking for but they do so with a subjective approach.

The first thing to consider is to have each position come with detailed job descriptions that highlight the required skills to complete the task (e.g. individuals employed in accounting need to be highly detailed).

The second is that every individual or potential employee must be evaluated based in terms of how personal qualities correspond to the needs for the position. (By its way of saying it should be done the same way for those who are transferred or made a promotion.)

The third step is that the differences should be noted, and either employees should be instructed on the skills that are lacking or someone else with the capabilities should be given the task to perform them. Everyone is not perfect. Everyone has flaws in our skills. What's important is to recognize that and adjusting for that.

What is the best way to prepare for an interview?

I've witnessed a number of potential employees interviewing incorrect approach. They sit down, and then have an enjoyable conversation. The interviewees are told all about their company, and then inquire about their personal lives. They review the resume, and then ask handful of questions. When asked questions about the applicant an interviewer might say something along the lines of "He's nice."

My typical response is "Good. We'd like to recruit the most pleasant people. Are they able to do the job?"

After the interview, the person who interviewed you will respond "Well, we had a great conversation."

Ahhh! Did you learn anything?

The procedure for interviews is identical for the majority of job descriptions. Before you go to the interview, glance through the description of your job, the abilities your applicant must be able to demonstrate and the other traits you think are worth mentioning. (I typically write these down on a paper notepad which I can refer to in an interview.) In the course of your interview, it is important to gain a broad perception of the candidate before you get into the specifics to find out how they measure up with these particular skills. Also, look a bit more deeply into the areas where there's a concern or doubt.

In the case of fundraising you must ensure that the fundraiser's candidate has a business plan in place that considers potential donors as well as existing ones are aware of the goods and services they are looking for and applies the right selling skills to the appropriate persons in the right numbers to reach the desired number of donors.

As you're never likely to recruit people who have previous experiences in fundraising (and even people who are experienced in working on the task could not be effective in doing them) It is important to take a look at the qualifications required to complete those jobs. There are four essential abilities for salespeople as well as fundraisers.

Intelligence. When you're fundraising, you're working with people who are successful. The fundraisers must decide about what questions they should inquire about, the best way to approach questions, and what their reply signifies. They, then would like to speak to somebody who understands all there is to know about the organisation and who can be able to answer any difficult questions.

An easy way to gauge intelligence is to look at what the students performed in their high school. If they had good marks and were smart, then they're intelligent. If they didn't it doesn't mean much. There are plenty of socially intelligent fundraisers that majored in dating, rugby, or drinking in bars. There are plenty of alternatives to assess the level of intelligence. Are they able to grasp things fast during the interview? Do they have a good way of processing data? Are their most successful achievements based on some challenge? I hope you'll be able to discern the process they use to think but also the things they are most proud of.

Self-starter. The most successful fundraisers know the steps they need to take and follow through with it. They'll make one last phone call or drop off another email before the time they finish their day. The people who do this seem to be on the move. I love fundraisers that create lists of things to do prior to the event so they will get a restful night's rest. I've often stated that I'd rather take the reins of the racehorse rather than try to pull the donkey.

Find out how candidates make themselves ready for the event. What are they most interested in do during their spare time? Are they an example to others?

Introspective. Fundraisers are often given a bad reputation for being confident and boastful. This is not true. People are extremely social However, the majority of us have a sense of insecurity. We are all insecure. It is important to stand out. We would like to have our identity on the wall. That's why I can understand the reckless, devil-may-care mindset But will the person ever learn? Will the individual evaluate their performance and abilities and implement the necessary adjustments in order to be better? What if the person's response to criticism be filled with excuses and arguments for why the events cannot be controlled by the fundraiser?

Find out about the weaknesses of people. Particularly, inquire about their mistakes as well as what they learnt from these. If they exclusively describe their strengths as flaws (e.g., "I work too hard") or they aren't willing to share their strengths details with you, then you might face a dilemma.

Aims to achieve goals. I'm not looking for someone who is willing to try. I'm looking for a person who can figure out the reason why something was wrong, and change their behaviour and complete the same task until the goal is reached. For me, goal-oriented does not just mean creating objectives. It is the process of try/fail/learn/succeed. I don't like to fail, however, not nearly in the same way as I want to be successful. If I make a mistake and learn, I want it to never repeat itself. However, I'll not be successful. In reality, I've been terribly wrong. The next one will be so satisfying.

An introspective approach helps to identify the weaknesses. The goal orientation helps to recalibrate and encourages you to take another shot. I enjoy looking for success as well as failings.

If I can identify a goal-oriented individual who is self-starting intelligent, shrewd, and self-aware I am convinced that I am a perfect candidate. The process of identifying skills and arranging interviews for required skills could be applied to any role.

In the process of interviewing, keep your eyes on the prize. You aren't likely to find someone that meets your needs. There were times that as a director of a company I was required to recruit an assistant or senior or a higher-level person. Since I don't like the routine, I'd search to hire someone with the additional skill of detail-oriented. In bringing these people on me, I was able to overcome my weaknesses and created an improved team. Before hiring new staff, consider how they'll fit into others on the group.

Managing Performance

If you ask a bunch of management colleagues what they dislike the most about their job and they'll almost always answer their performance reviews. Why? There is a great deal of details. Managers aren't sure which document to use in the absence of written expectations and communication throughout. Infrequently, employees get the manager's view prior to the meeting, this creates a tension scenario. However, it does not have to be. Actually, if the supervisor does everything right, a formal review of performance can be put out of the window, and replaced with scores, a regular evaluation of the metrics and on. It is recommended that the employee attends this event and discusses what the successes and problems can be found.

The position has a description. The worker should be assessed on how well they perform in accordance with the requirements of the job. Any deficiencies should be identified. Regularly meet on measures, and ask questions about what progress was made or not realized. The last part of this piece is to repair or enhance the areas that do not meet the standards. A manager could introduce more awareness, training or even a shift of the procedure or expectation. Include a touch of affection and concern for how they are doing to become an effective boss!

Implementing it

1. Have Integrity and practice humbleness.

2. Develop goals and strategies that are realistic in order to reach the goals of both the team as well as every individual. It's crucial to have everyone's participation and adhering in the final plan. (Plus this takes part of the responsibility off of you.)

3. Identify the abilities required for the job and evaluate the person in charge's capabilities in relation to these abilities. When hiring an employee for the first time, review applicants in relation to the abilities needed.

4. Identify the best way to improve the abilities needed to complete your job or address weaknesses.

5. Frequently update status on the performance of both teams and individuals.

6. Find positive things you can use, and then say them.

7. Hold individuals accountable for the goals they have set and to correct them privately.

8. Love Your Team.

Chapter 8: Leadership

Being a business owner I wanted my staff to be motivated and have a sense mission. The goal was to transform the world, and we would have enjoyable in the process. I bought a table for pool in the breakroom area, handed the shirts away and other things featuring the company's logo in them. We also had an entire fridge with complimentary sodas. It was unfortunate that, although they were enthused about environmental issues, not all of my employees were looking to be a part of changing the world. They were mostly happy with their jobs, however their primary purpose was to make ends meet. There were employees who had bad attitude and some had to be dismissed. Why was this? It's more than just simple things like following the rules.

It was a frantic business that relied on software. It was imperative to move forward and everyone had to play their part.

My responsibility was to not just provide direction, but also to inspire. I was forced to consider, "How do I get everyone to be productive?"

In a lot of nonprofits leadership, it is assumed that everybody is in their mission and, as such that they don't have to feel driven. The most stressed, unappreciated and overworked employees I've ever encountered have been employed in non-profit organizations.

The leader of a charity is highly motivated due to the personal commitment of their employees and a sense of belonging. But, this kind of leader often isn't aware that how important the rest of the staff are. They expect their staff members to be energized simply by the fact that their charity feeds the homeless and bringing people to Christ or whatever the goal has to be.

Martin Chemers, in his book An Integrative Theory for Leadership, described the term "leadership" as "the method of social influence through where one individual can solicit the assistance and help of other people in the achievement of a task."[1]

If the management assists an employee to understand what they should do, the leader, in turn will explain the reason why. There are a variety of traits and characteristics of a great leader. We will focus on three: trust the vision, trust, and communications.

Trust

Just like a successful manager, trust is crucial to a leader. Apart from being honest the leader should demonstrate confidence by showing concern for the employees.

A big part of trust comes from the employees feeling they are getting your help. They want to know they can talk to their supervisor and express a grievance and ask questions or ask for help. I often told my staff that one of my primary responsibilities was to assist them in removing obstacles to their progress. If you claim this, then you have to follow the rules. It's about doing exactly what you said you would perform.

Everyone wants to feel appreciated. Giving employees a good treatment is not simply nice but also efficient. Therefore, take time to spend with employees. Ask questions. Listen. Make notes. One popular method is to manage through walking. However, don't simply wander around. Engage. Be sincere. Find the truth. The actions you take will increase trust in your team's ability to take charge.

However, that's not enough. If the leader is caring but doesn't have the necessary skills, an worker could still be able to make a move to disengage the leader. Another way employees fall off their faith is if managers fail to deal with employees who are in trouble or when they face situations. People will be skeptical of an employee who is unable to take action.

Vision

A great leader can help employees see the potential for success by presenting the goals, strategy and the goals of the company. If the operational and strategic plan are in place then employees will be able to be able to see how their work connects to the company's vision. Vision is comprised of these:

1. Understanding reality. The biggest obstacle for understanding the reality of things is the pride. I don't know how many times I've spoken to executives who claimed to have the right answers, regardless of what the factual evidence suggests. A leader who is humble can doubt the conclusions, solicit input from others and then to think about the findings. It can also be strengthened by collecting data and

analyzing the previous activities similar to this.

2. Seeing the consequences. This is a bit more difficult to master. Conceptual people are able to think of concepts but require guidance to link the dots to the final result. People with a keen eye can perceive the process but can forget about the end outcome and become distracted by the finer details.

This doesn't mean that they aren't part of their job. But they might not be aware of what their particular jobs contribute to worth, or, even more importantly, they may not realize that their job is crucial because they are an intermediary stage prior to when someone other person performs the service. An appropriate response would be "The purpose behind doing what we do is because it allows for us to ...," to "Jenny the great job we do with customer service implies the that ...."

Your employees do not simply need to know how they are a part of the plan, they need to understand how your company is fulfilling its goals. In addition to for-profit businesses the employees of nonprofit organizations are keen to know if they are moving forward.

Communication

It is essential to have a strategic plan that you inform all employees. Many managers don't share the plan since they aren't convinced that their employees need the entire information needed for their work: "He's a forklift operator for heaven's sake!" It's true that if employees are aware of their the mission of their organization, they will feel more strongly about their mission, feel more focused and in tune with other members of the team.

An effective leader is always in contact. Make sure to publish your business plan with as much detail as can be considered sensible. Post it on the site of your company's internal website; make copies available to those who would like to read it. Or you can even upload an PowerPoint overview to your internal site; allow people to understand the goals and the criteria to be assessed. The most effective way to present your vision is to begin with a description of what you as a team created the strategy and what assumptions you made. Tell them what you plan to do in order to verify these assumptions and the kind of actions that could be taken if it goes either way or another. Continue this by organizing the location or department as well as gatherings in which you repeat the tale. It is necessary to repeat the narrative and fill in any holes. In addition, employees could ask questions now that they've considered. Listen. You may be amazed by certain of the comments.

The strategy must be reasonable. It is important to not only understand the logic behind your strategy, but they should also feel that there's a high likelihood of the expected outcomes taking place. There are times when people require an even more precise step-by-step process for how the events will occur. Sometimes they have to recognize that the person in charge is competent, has the ability and willpower to get plans happen. It is essential to come up with an organized plan that you're able to communicate all areas that need to be addressed. Make sure to meet with your team regularly and provide them with a status report. If you've given them realistic goals, then show them how much progress has taken place. If your plans weren't realistic or unforeseen circumstances made it impossible to meet those goals, let your team! Discuss what you expected to take place and how it actually took place. Discuss what you plan to change so that you can get back on the right track. Remember, realistic, attainable goals are crucial for success.

They want to know to know the truth. They are able to detect a falsehood or cover-up which means you've completely lost credibility. But that doesn't mean you should say "All is gone. The company will need to dismiss everyone by June, unless we can turn things around." An alternative is to recognize the seriousness of the issue and draw a picture of the way you intend get the results you want.

The past couple of years there's been a lot of organizations and non-profits which have experienced tumultuous change. Many have shut down or experienced major layoffs, adjustments to the way they operate, restructuring as well as any other issue you can imagine. It is therefore reasonable to assume that employees were hesitant, concerned about their work perhaps even seeking new opportunities elsewhere. When I consult with businesses that are facing difficult times, I have often told them "Employees don't leave when bad things happen; they leave when they don't see a way out of the bad things."

If the company experienced an awful year, with massive loss and staff reductions, yet the CEO explained why adjustments were needed and also helped employees envision how the business will be able to succeed in the coming years, odds that they'll fight it through and remain committed. Two conditions apply: (1) that the employees concur with the chief in these matters as well (2) that employees are confident that the leadership team can actually accomplish these tasks. They must trust that the team of management will execute their plan.

Can You Teach Visualization?

Should a leader capable of visualizing? Absolutely, vision is crucial. Many founders of technology businesses aren't experts in the field of technology. They are able to see the business (i.e. what it takes to manage a business and serve clients) however; they aren't expert in the field of product.

Are you able to train people to imagine? Sure, but as with any art, it will take several years of practicing. In the second part of this guide, we'll look at how you can create the business plan which contains the goal and methods to achieve it.

Good leaders look at his staff. If the leader is leader or not, the manager seeks suggestions, pushes employees to think outside the boundaries, and depends on experts in the field to guide the team. Self-confidence is the place to come into. A leader who is courageous to declare, "I don't know, but collectively, we can figure it out." The team will be grateful to the boss for doing that.

In the event of a situation in which you're not sure what to do, consult your colleagues and explain to them about the situation. Ask them for help in resolving the issue. As I've seen it I've yet hear anyone say, "You are the boss. You should know!" Instead, they wanted more specific information on the issue we were trying to address and what requirements were imposed on solving the problem.

As the boss is still a must to trust in the solutions. Still, you must visualize that it is running. It is still up to you to decide whether or not whether or not you want to proceed. This is where your business plan plays a role. Are there assumptions or strategies you've discussed and think are the most feasible ways to go? As a CEO I'd talk with the company's board members about the plans we were making and the best way to accomplish the goals, as well as what our beliefs were. If they agreed with these ideas, I'd revisit them following the time they had tried the ideas and tell them, "Hey, the things we thought were likely to occur didn't take place. Instead, this is what transpired. What we have took away from it and that is what we're going to follow up on." Do you think that this means that if you adhere to these instructions, you won't get terminated for failing to meet the goals you set for yourself? No. Executives are often fired due to failing, regardless of the fact that it was their fault or not. This approach reduces the chance of surprises and can help build an understanding of the same vision, usually leading to shared accountability.

Get People Involved

I've been labeled a driver. It happened a few times. I'm a very action-oriented. I once had someone come to my workplace and told me, "I'd like you to contact the Mr. X and talk about ..." prior to everything else the phone was out and dialed the number. My employee turned around and said, "Could you at least wait until I tell you what I'd like you to talk to him about?"

This is because I am inclined to think things through to do things by myself. In order to be a successful leader, it is essential to get your team members to assist you in coming to the right solution. It is possible to think of the solution, after that, I'll recite the Gettysburg Address in my head as they think about the problem, but I make sure to remain silent until they finish the calculation and share the outcome with me.

When they reach an end, I will try to persuade them to join. Are they convinced that this is possible? Do they think this is the way things will take place? What could we do to improve the chances of this happening? occur? Making sure that the executives be a part of the process and to take ownership is the essential action.

Building trust by engaging with others as well as communicating their plans and showing a consistent achievement of the goals set, employees will become more productive happy, engaged and more productive at work.

Implementing it

1. Be explicit about your goal. Create a mission statement in writing which is explained in chapter 4. Each employee should be aware of the purpose of the mission and what the mission. Discuss how the business will be successful as well as the measures you'll use to evaluate the effectiveness of the company.

2. Help employees comprehend their roles and the responsibilities they have to fulfill. Set reasonable goals for them to measure the performance. Provide them with training or assist with training so that they can improve their performance. No matter what, employees must be able to perform their job. (see chapters 7 and 7, namely, metrics.)

3. Build trust. Maintain integrity. Praise. It's so easy. The uber-dedicated boss may not

realize the need for encouragement which we all need. Humans are vulnerable beings. It is easier to perform when we're rewarded and told to act in the right way. Be consistent with what you have said you will accomplish. Keep track of your progress.

4. Get employees to be involved. Some employees don't show much emotion. They're usually the calm and quiet ones who could exist because of an interest in the cause. Find this kind of employee engaged by asking questions on ways to meet certain objectives or tasks.

5. Communicate often. Inform people of the company's accomplishments. Send progress reports. Make sure to demonstrate how each individual's or department is impacted by the overall organization's efficiency.

1. An Integrative Theory of Leadership, Martin Chemers, P. 5, 1997

Chapter 9: The Board Of Directors

The directors' board might be the most vital component of your organization. The function of the board of directors is to collaborate together with the executive director in establishing direction, and also to make sure that laws are adhered to and that practices adhere to ethical standards.

The most important task for the board is to select and the evaluation of the director's executive. The selection process can be a difficult task!

The board is legally obligation to ensure decision-making is made to the good of the charity, not any gain for staff or board members. The board does this through reviewing their plans and making decisions, and also seeking legal counsel from an attorney.

The board typically spends its time in ensuring sustainability via efficient allocation of resources. In chapter 7

"Developing a Strategic Plan," the board must assist in defining the implementation of the plan by analyzing and suggesting the best possible utilization of resources. The majorities of board members are significant donors or have the ability to have influence over others to give.

Choosing Board Members

I've spent many hours trying to get board members who are not the right ones and then trying to remove those people off, then trying to bring the correct people to join. Board members need to contribute something to the table. What should you be looking for?

My opinion is that the most crucial element is someone that acts as a sounding-board for the executive director regarding the financial aspects. Someone that has prior experience in a variety of subjects covered in this book. An enormous help to me in the beginning of my business was my principal investor Chuck Johnson. I would have meetings with Chuck about what I believed I had to accomplish and the best way to do it. Chuck would openly discuss with me the strengths and drawbacks of the strategy. He would get deeper and explain the dangers of every strategy. He would advise me to be cautious when I was a bit bold ... after a the second look, he had didn't think that I was bold enough! When I was going through a very difficult time, Chuck suggested that he together with me meet every week in my office to discuss the expectations and plans for the week, and look at the actual outcomes and decide what we could do to change our plans in order to maximize efficiency. Chuck was instrumental in saving the business.

Avoid sycophants. Nothing frustrates more than having plans presented and the entire team simply nodding. I can remember sitting before a whiteboard and thinking how much time. People simply want me to repair things and stay informed. Thus, you must find those who are interested. They must possess an interest in the project and be willing to contribute an amount of money for the venture, or have an expertise in particular that will be beneficial to the team.

Before they decide to commit, if they are willing to give me a single day in a month. It means that I want people to be more than just attending the board meetings, but also to take part in a committee or helping us raise funds.

The Board Meeting

The board meetings must be scheduled every quarter to examine the plan's assumptions and its implementation the strategy and also to assess the best and most effective utilization of the resources in the future. As such, the board can provide advice or provides services that assist the management team.

The board isn't operational board. This means that the board is not regularly meeting and analyzing Coke sales (this is what happened to one board I served on.) The purpose of the board meetings isn't intended to re-evaluate the executive director's or the management team. The board is not able to manage any person other than an executive director. If the director isn't doing a good job and the board is concerned, it should take discipline in the event that sub-par performance persists; the board has to remove the director. However, don't allow the board to dictate how the task will be accomplished. If you're seeing this it's likely that you have the wrong the wrong board member.

The majority of nonprofit statutes require for the board to be able to approve the budget. The board is required to hear about the plans; accept the results and assumptions as likely as they are; and then make changes to the budget as needed.

Board meetings every quarter should serve as a review of progress and to provide advice to the management.

It's time to put it into practice

1. Does your board contain members with the experience and expertise to take the right decision-making decisions that will benefit your company?

2. What are you missing?

a. Financial advisor?

b. Several major gift donors?

c. Subject matter expertise?

3. Do the members of the board know what they are expected to do in their responsibilities? Are they fully committed to their work and contributing efficiently?

Chapter 10: Compare A Non-Profit Charity To A For-Profit Business

For a better understanding of the distinctions between a profit-making company and a non-profit charitable organization and when these differences become obvious in the pursuit of cash, take this into consideration:

A business that is for profit is a financial choice in which the investor hopes to generate profits from the investments at least the amount of money that he could earn from other investments, like an account in a savings bank or the purchasing a share shares in the NYSE.

The basis for any investment payback or payment by the company to an investor is the earnings from the company. If the business makes an income, it may make the investor pay back on the stake.

However, they have been designed to not generate any profits whatsoever. So, any contributor or investor in a nonprofit enterprise will be motivated by something other aside from a profit in cash from the investment. The job of the person who is organizing of a non-profit organization is to identify what types of satisfaction or benefits you can offer to the donors to take the place of any potential cash gain.

This book explains how you can achieve that feat.

But, be aware that the non-profit charitable organization seeking funds must present plans that include several of the same discussion and projections that are typically included in a business plan for profit.

There is a possibility that the plan of an organization that is not for profit must be more clear and convincing as compared to a business for profit plan, precisely because the outcomes will be evaluated in non-monetary measures.

Additionally, a business plan is essential when it comes to a non-profit business as opposed to a conventional enterprise, as it is not able to count sales revenues as the main source of funding for its operations. Additionally, even if you are able to fund all the initial costs and continuing costs of your business It is a important idea to create an outline of your business before you even begin to write checks as it helps keep you focused.

The principle of an established, profitable business plan is the creation of an estimation of the earnings the company will earn from offering products or services to clients and compare that to the expected cost for providing those goods or services, and then determine if there will remain any funds in the form of an income.

It's an easy idea to make enough money to cover the items that you offer and perhaps there's a little extra for you, and to repay the loan that you get from other people for the start of your venture.

Whether you are the business owner need funds from people in order to start and manage your non-profit business or finance your entire business without assistance when you invest in a new company is a commercial investment: Investors deposit funds and hope they will get back the investment, and generate an income also.

NON-PROFIT PLAN

Perhaps, you're confident that a certain item or service is beneficial to those who really need it. You could also have identified a social issue which is normally the job of a tax-paying government bureau, yet the it is not able to provide the money to fulfill the requirement.

The individuals who will benefit by your initiative will not be able to afford your service or product due to a variety of motives.

If this were a profit-making company, then the absence of revenues would cause problems What if you get money for the opening of your company if you aren't generating those profits that allow you to return the investment?

This is how you can fix this issue for your charity that is non-profit.

Look for those with whom you already agree that you have a need.

A few of them will support your ideas! Most of them aren't expecting to get paid!

It is then your responsibility to convince others who are of the conviction you have that you will identify specific goals to achieve your common goal.

It is possible to accomplish this by describing clearly and the specific steps you'll take in order to provide actions or products which meet the needs. It's exactly what your non-profit venture's strategy is designed to achieve.

When you're looking to start here's the best way to complete the initial step:

FIRST STEP - DESCRIBE YOUR ORGANIZATION

Before you begin to ask people for cash You must write an entire outline of the things your company is going to do, who they will be entrusted with and what the cost will be to accomplish those tasks.

If this sounds just as a business plan, that's because it's exactly an ordinary business plan. One major difference is the fact that your business will not generate a profit, consequently, you and it are dependent on the generosity of donors to cover the expenses.

DESCRIBE THE ORGANIZATION

Find out what a formal business description will look like for a non-profit company prior to writing the non-profit's description. Go to Chapter 3, Selecting the Right business, and describe Your Business pages 27 through 31'How to Create the Business Plan Paperback 13th Edition or pages 29 to 34 How to write the Business Plan Paperback 12th edition. This will give you an understanding of many of the questions you'll be asked when you write your non-profit proposal.

A lot, but not all of the principles and activities discussed in "How to Write a Business Plan', paperback 13th Edition as well as 12th Edition. The book is also applicable to non-profit businesses. While reading the other sections of this book make sure you remember that I'm using the term "business" as a reference to either a profit-making enterprise or charity. It's helpful to comprehend the way a business for profit writes an operating plan, even if some of the ideas may not be relevant to the charitable organisation you run. As an example, many of the ideas related to profits margins and sales revenue won't be used in your business plan.It is important to understand that

The ebook contains illustrations of two fictional as well as distinct non-profit groups that are working to combat the impact of climate change. Once you've completed the chapters of Chapter 3"How to write an Effective Business Plan Paperback 13th Edition or 12th edition on for-profit companies, you're prepared to write the business description of your business.

MISSION STATEMENT

The description of your non-profit venture should be based on the Mission Statement. Simply put, your Mission Statement is a SHORT description of the goals you're doing with your new project. Also, the business description describes how the new nonprofit can fulfill your goal.

Here's an example mission statement of one of the fictional charities listed in the appendix. The mission of this venture is to cut down on the effects of global warming through plant trees. The name is Greens!.

Greens! The mission may be written as this:

MISSION STATEMENT: GREENS!

Greens! goal is to minimize greenhouse gas emissions that occur in the Earth's atmosphere through plant as many trees as possible in the forest areas around the world.

If you were in your position it would be your responsibility to add a description of the steps your team will take to achieve the goal.

The next stage in creating your own description is to select between two models for non-profits either old-fashioned as well as 21st Century. A little background information will assist you with your selection.

Chapter 11: History And Types Of Non-Profits

In writing your proposal when you write your plan, you should select either of the two styles of organization for your plan. Choose a traditional classic model, or an old-fashioned one. Or you could choose a more modern model that has an 21st Century structure; the modern model is based on measurable, specific actions you are able to accomplish to achieve your goals.

When it was the time of the old-fashioned charitable organizations, the tax exempt granted to donors was sufficient for people who had extra funds to contribute in order to get the tax credits. So long as the organization presented a convincing argument for the issue they wanted to solve The donor would be happy in the knowledge that they had been making a difference through their funds.

The majority of donors were content by general discussion of their charitable work and infrequent financial statements. A business plan could include a list of fundamentals and an explanation of the way in which the charity will take action to address the issue.

There are the examples of business plans that fit these types in the following paragraphs, beginning on page 7.

SECOND STEP - FORECAST CASH NEEDS

Whatever model you select, you must create a budget of the expenses you incur in cash and any needed donations. It's a big process and requires is a significant amount of effort. This is the goal to calculate the amount of money you'll have to begin and sustain the organization.

The basic elements of any plan can be found in commercial companies in greater specific detail in Chapters 3 through 9 in 'How to Create a Business Plan' Paperback 13th

Edition, as well as the 12th edition. If you are having difficulty with any aspect of the proposal for your non-profit organization, look up the appropriate section in those chapters. Then, you can adapt the elements of the for-profit business plan will be required to write your nonprofit plan.

I highly recommend you go through the entire text particularly Chapters 3 to 9 on 'How to Write an Effective Business Plan Paperback 13th edition or 12th edition. Before you start making your plan for non-profit - the rest of your life will become easier.

In either regular business or a nonprofit goal at the beginning is to figure out the amount of money you'll have to raise to launch and maintain your business.

The funds can be used to establish the business, rent an office, purchase computers and desks, and develop an online presence in addition to paying each month for the expenses of running an business.

For a start on this task, refer to Chapter 6 of Your Profit and Loss Forecast "How to Write an Effective Business Plan Paperback 13th Edition, or 12th Edition that explains the fundamentals of forecasting your income and expenses in a monthly manner for all businesses. Non-profit organizations will have to fill out the application. There is a difference in that nonprofits don't generate a lot of income from its activities, but must cover all costs for supporting the organization.

The line for revenue at the top of the form has been replaced with a line of expected donations for nonprofits instead of revenue. This line was located on the bottom of the form, for non-profits of this chapter for reasons of practicality.

Also, make sure to take the time to read Chapter 7, Your Cash Flow Forecast and

Capital Expenditure Plan "How to Create an Effective Business Plan paperback 13th edition or 12th edition. The chapter outlines the fundamental ways you can prepare the forecasts described in the previous paragraphs. These concepts are the same in both companies. The two plans for non-profit organizations in the following sections address these concerns and alter the responses for the same non-profit as the one you have.

FINDING REAL PEOPLE TO GIVE YOU MONEY

If you've determined the amount of funds you'll require, you can begin presenting your idea to real people, and then asking them to make donations. Don't shy away from asking for donations. If you've ever made or donated to a worthwhile organization, then you've probably been approached by letters asking for more contributions from your. The letters can range from asking for money to threats of extortion. Potential donors are likely to expect excitement from those who ask for money. They may also consider good manners, or even insecurity as absence of dedication!

For the first step to begin, you must read Chapter 4. Possible sources of money to start or expand your Small Business, beginning on the page 65 in 'How to write the Business Plan paperback 13th Edition, or page 61 "How to write an Effective Business Plan,' paperback 12th Edition for suggestions regarding how you can find supporters for your business. Look particularly at the section called supporters on page 83 of thirteenth Ed. or page 80 in 12th Ed. or 80 for the 12th Ed. avoid the section on Loans and Equity Investments page from 66 to 76 in the 13th Ed. and 63-74 within the 12th Ed. There is a benefit already since you have the ability to write the names of groups or individuals that are interested by your belief. If you do not have this list, you'll have to make it. Make use of

Google to find groups and people who are able to are in agreement with your objectives. Also, check out the other information at the conclusion of this Appendix, the book about raising money written by Ilona Bray, founder of Nolo Press.

Additionally, you're an excellent way to start conversations as you're trying to aid individuals instead of merely making a profit. Your personal connections, which are listed in Chapter 4, "How to Create an Effective Business Plan paperback 13th Edition as well as 12th Edition are helpful as they will help other people or help a cause through funding for your business.

When you've compiled some prospective donors, it's crucial that you have a detailed program in hand. It must be clear what you'll accomplish. This is more crucial for you than in a typical, for-profit company.

The plan will show anyone who is who is interested in your help that your thought process has been thorough and you've considered the essential details required to realize your dream. The non-profit's business plan is your sales tool to convince supporters that your concept is viable. It outlines precisely what you'll accomplish, as well as the amount it will take to accomplish these things.

ASKING FOR MONEY - YOUR ADVANTAGE: TAX DEDUCTIONS FOR DONORS

For you to find funds To help you locate money IRS of all places helps you to get this funds. Donations made to a well-organized non-profit organization can be tax deductible to the donor or investor!

It is possible to give your investors as well as donors tax-free deductions in the simple act of arranging your business following IRS regulations. This is as simple as it gets.

Tax deductions aren't the sole reason why people invest in a venture However, it definitely aids.

The basics of tax deductions:

You'll need to be classified as to be a"501 (c) organization from the IRS. A designation of 501(c) indicates that the company is a business that has an income tax exemption that is available to donation donors. Also, a person who makes a donation of money or other important items to a tax exempt entity can claim the deduction of income tax in their tax return for the cash amount of the gift. Other small benefits that are available through government agencies like the Federal Government.

Furthermore, a recognized non-profit organization is not obliged to be liable for Federal or State tax on income revenue. The extra funds can be rolled forward to next year's fiscal year. Shortfalls also make it necessary for the non-profit to reduce costs or increase contributions in some way.

The most popular kind of tax-exempt non-profit organisation falls within the category

501(c)(3) in which an organization that is nonprofit is exempt from taxation under the federal taxation if the activities are for the following reasons that are religious, charitable and educational, scientific, test for the sake of security of the public, encouraging competitive sports for amateurs, or protecting children from cruelty or animals. It is important to note that the 501(c)(4) as well as 501(c)(6) categories pertain to organizations that are politically active. They have grown in importance since the election in 2004 for president. '[IRS Form 990]

If you're thinking of creating a non-profit entity that is subject to IRS 501(c) regulations the best option is working closely with a lawyer or CPA to ensure that all your t's have been crossed and your i's have been crossed. If you do not fill out the forms correctly it could cause donors to face tax-related issues and possibly criminal charges too.

Also, see How to Form a Non-Profit Corporation, Anthony Mancuso, Nolo Press for guidance. It is applicable to all states and clarifies the legal responsibilities that must be followed when forming an exempt from taxation, non-profit company. I provide a few basics concerning corporate ownership and organization in Chapter 4, Potential Financial Sources, Corporations and Red Tape on page 75titled "How to write the Business Plan paperback 13th Edition, or on page 72, "How to write an Business Plan in a Paperback 12th edition.

Chapter 12: Board Of Directors

One of the steps for forming a 501[C]3 company is determining a small number of members to join the board of directors. Although the code of corporations generally does not need a huge committee, a lot of organizations utilize Board membership to provide a reason to attract donors. Some organizations even require that Board members pay annual fees in exchange for membership.

It is advisable to think about the composition and role of the Board of Directors you have cautiously. Since each Board members is personally responsible to all errors and mistakes of the business. This is why a lot of Board members may ask that you purchase insurance in order to safeguard them against claims as a condition of their employment. Additionally, they'll expect from you that you remain fully informed about the actions you take as the CEO.

Your Board will help you achieve your goals when they're qualified; however the Board could destroy your whole company if they're not the appropriate choice.

This is how the chief executive officer of an old organization called 501(C) 3 described it:

The members of a Board in any company are like the foundation of the structure, because if the cornerstone is broken or faulty, the entire structure the work that was done might fall to the ground.

It is crucial it is essential that Board members are with a reputation for integrity with a genuine determination to see the cause flourish. It's also beneficial having leadership qualities as well as fundraising skills and experience in the field of grants writing.

It is important to pay attention to existing relationships with Board members. If a Board member is bound by another member of the board and there's a risk of being in the situation where you are forced to accept any demands or even lose the business completely.

Diedre Williams, April 2017. The CEO of the homeless shelter for teens for five years.

Make sure you are careful in selecting Board members since you'll require their assistance and knowledge. Since you're the person in charge of the Board You will gain by having a better awareness of their responsibilities and rights. The book below has helped many CEO's as well as Board members to understand their role and responsibilities:

The game's rules Inside the corporate boardroom Hardcover 1984; by Thomas L Whisler (Author) ISBN-10: 0870944630. ISBN-13 0870944635 ISBN

A significant part of overseeing the organisation every day is to seek approval from the Board to take any actions you want to and keep them updated on your activities. Be aware that the Board is likely to require documents proving specific results from the organization since they are legally accountable for the charitable organization. That's why CPA and attorney can be of great help. CPA and lawyer can assist in ensuring that the procedures are in place.

Also read: Managing the Nonprofit Organisation, Paperback 9 May 2006 written by Peter F. Drucker (Author), HarperBusiness

SAMPLE BUSINESS PLANS: OLD-TIMEY, and MODERN

Two different plans are offered here. Both provide information about organizations that are working to combat global warming.

The first represents an older-style non-profit that is dependent on publicity and conferences in order to enhance the quality of Earth's atmosphere. The other is a contemporary non-profit that chooses specific actions it could take in order to lower global temperatures.

EXAMPLE 1: OLD-TIMEY NON-PROFIT PLAN

Here's an illustration of a traditional charity entirely fictional, obviously. Imagine a charity wants to contribute positively in reducing the effects of global warming.

The charity is referred to as The World Of Warming, or WOW as an acronym.

The business plan could mention the various workshops and conferences WOW recommends as a strategy to reduce global warming. WOW will also provide some information regarding its founding members and Board members. As WOW is a business and is a corporation, the Board is responsible for choosing how to spend the donations to ensure that they conform with the plan of business.

To learn how to write the resumes of your founders and other important employees, refer to Chapter 5 Your Financial Statement and Resume Draft Your Business's Accomplishment The section on resumes begins on page 100 of the book 'How to write the Business Plan that is a paperback 13th edition or page 98 in 'How to Create an Business Plan Paperback 12th edition. The likelihood is that an individual financial statement will not be necessary as you are unlikely to need a loan, however, if you do require it, then the remainder in Chapter 5 "How to Write an Business Plan and Paperback 13th Edition and 12th edition explain how to create an appropriate one.

Carefully write this part because prospective donors are likely to base their decisions on the organization.

Check out Exhibit A to get the first year's profit and forecasts for WOW using the old model.

In this instance, the Cash Flow Statement and the Profit and Loss statement are both the same. Most non-profits don't need separate accounts and this appendix provides two non-profit examples in which this is the case. If you are concerned that you may incur accruals that differ from cash account balances, consider reading Chapter 7 of Your Cash Flow Forecast as well as Capital and Capital spending Plan that begins at page 158 of the book "How to Write a Corporate Plan,' paperback 13th Edition, or page 153 from 'How To Create the Business Plan Paperback 12th edition. Talk to the advice of a CPA for any questions regarding how to create this section.

The plan then outlines the costs for salaries, rent, and utilities and the exact costs for presenting the conferences and workshops. If you need help estimating cost of future expenditures like the cost of utilities and rent, check out Chapter 6: Your Profit and Loss forecast, Section 4 Fixed Expenses starting on page 139, 'How to Create the Business Plan Paperback 13th edition or page 136 "How to Create the Business Plan paperback 12th edition.

The total amount of your annual expenses is the WOW's goal for fundraising throughout the entire year. This projection, together with description and explanations becomes the Plan you give to potential donors.

Potential donors may have a personal meeting with WOW's President Dr. Norman Slick; in that conversation Slick asks for donations. Slick asks for donations.

If annual fundraising is not enough to meet the target, WOW simply reduces some of the activities proposed so that the actual expenses are in line with amount of money raised.

If WOW has received more contributions than the amount projected in the previous year, WOW will record an excess that can be utilized for the following year's events; this will reduce the amount of fundraising for next year's. So, WOW may have donations over and, in contrast, lower than expenses, however, it wouldn't have gains or losses that could be assessed from the IRS or the state income tax authorities.

In the past, certain non-profits have their own money for different actions they engage in. If your business will be operating with distinct funds, they requires the assistance of CPA CPA in order to set up and manage these funds. This article is limited to a brief discussion of donations, revenues and expenditures only.

Chapter 13: Non-Profit Plan With 21st Century Deliverables - Greens!

The times have certainly changed.

Nowadays, many of those who have extra funds also are surrounded by accountants and lawyers to ensure that money is spent effectively. When they say 'effectively' typically, they mean that they wish to know the items they spend their money on and verify that the person who receives it GREENS!! - is actually doing some real thing with the cash.

As the years progress, people need to know what they are spending their money on. It's no longer enough to mention speeches delivered and the conferences that were attended as the only item of the company.

This means that the charities are expected to produce tangible results that can be tracked in some time.

Your job is to design these quantifiable activities and are known as "deliverables," which is abbreviation.

In essence, a deliverable can be described as a particular event that a charitable organization can do that is recorded as well as tracked over time that will also help the mission of the charity.

The job of writing the strategy is to link the actions you outline as "deliverables" directly with the goals of the company. Because the goal of Greens! is to limit the global temperature, they decide to grow more trees within the forest to be a way in achieving its goal. The details of this are discussed in the following paragraphs.

TWO CLASSES OF DELIVERABLES

There are generally two different types of deliverables utilized by charitable organisations.

The first is that some charities rely entirely on donations to generate source of income. They do not receive any funds from other organizations by performing the task they have been assigned. This is the principle the 21st century's Greens! was derived from.

There are also charities who receive funds by an outside company that is based on the accomplishment of a particular action.

Perhaps, for instance, the charity assists in providing psychotherapy to victims of rape in cities that provide public funding for this purpose. The charity may be established to identify the rape victims to complete the paperwork required by the city, and retain counselors that provide the therapy. The charity will receive a payment by the city upon successful registration as well as after every counseling session.

If your nonprofit relies on payments from different entities, you'll need specify exactly how this program operates. Additionally, it's probably best to have any documentation provided by the other entity that outlines the conditions and terms under that the payments will take place.

INCORPORATING DELIVERABLES INTO A MODERN BUSINESS PLAN

To understand the concept of generating a product, look at how our current global warming group Greens! Greens! It does it. Let's say that Greens! opts to safeguard the forests of rain for its mission to cut down on the global temperature.

Maybe one particular and tangible greens! could do is grow tree species in the forest or to save trees that are already in the forest from being cut down.

In this case, it is essential to present an explanation of the reason Greens! decides to take the action of preserving and/or planting trees. The donors will need to believe that the delivery option chosen will be successful in achieving the purpose of delaying global warming, if the delivery can be successfully completed.

For background, you've discovered that planting trees can lessen global warming because it removes CO2 from the air. Though some researchers question the validity of this strategy but you've decided to pursue it regardless of the opinion pieces which suggests the opposite.

In this debate in this debate, we set Greens! the goal of saving existing trees and planting new trees in the amount of 11,000 total trees each year that is saved or planted within the rain forest for the next ten years. This will result in the total of 110,000 trees in 10 years. Although it may seem repeated, be aware that of the terms and figures utilized in this scenario are completely fictional and have no connection to the reality.

The planting of trees will be planned in this manner: Greens! is planning to plant 9,980 trees, at a amount of 833 trees each month for an overall direct cost [$2.00 cost of purchase for each tree and $3.00 direct labor costs to plant each tree to a cost amount of $5.00 per tree] $49,980 and the cost of office expenses, which is $60,000 for an overall direct cost for planting without overhead of $109,980 which is $11.02 for each tree that is that is planted. Because the planting of trees is Greens! principal activity, all costs of office overhead are attributed to this particular activity.

It's helpful to create a document in which you describe precisely how this plan will be executed. It should also include the resumes of those who are essential as well as the background of any people you'll hire for the job.

Additionally, Greens! may prevent further forests from getting cut up, by purchasing the land to create an area of nature reserve. Imagine you Greens! could acquire 100 acres of natural rain forest for an investment of $50,000 (or $500/acre) and that every acre is home to at least 10 trees to be preserved. It would imply that the purchase of the land could save 1000 trees for an average price 50 dollars per tree.

The section on land acquisition is required for common real estate documents like appraisals as well as surveys of the property that will be purchased.

If the total cost did not exceed the anticipated target for fund-raising, it is possible that the number of trees that are expected to be planted or saved could be altered. If the overall costs required for achieving the annual goal of 10,000 trees was less than its budget by say, $50,000, it is possible that the organization will surpass the goals it set. This means that the contributors are able to accomplish more than were expecting.

As the CEO, you must create the business plan with a projection of saving or planting 11,000 tree annually at a price of $160,000.

In the end, $160,000 in total costs each year is the fundraising goal for the organization. The charity must get from donors the entire amount projected for its expenses to achieve its objectives and deliver the 11,000 trees annually.

Check out Exhibit B to get the monthly forecast of expenditures and donations receipts that form the basis of this brand new template business plan.

It is then possible for the donor to claim the donation of $160,000 resulted in the distribution of 10,996 trees for an actual price that is $14.56 per tree ($160,000 of cost divided by 10,996 trees.

The Business Plan includes a total donation of $160,000 with an overall cost of $159,980. The donations surpass costs by

$20.00. We wish that they utilize their money in a wise way.

Thus, Greens! shows that the cost of planting trees is $11.02 per tree. However, the purchase of the land and saving trees on the new land is $50.00 for each tree. Tree planting is more cost efficient per tree, however buying land may make it more difficult to save trees as well as further Greens! goals.

Be aware that the entire story is fiction. However, readers can comprehend the concept that donors are seeking concrete, quantifiable results. And charitable organizations that are successful will devise methods to deliver the result. The most successful charities will show the way each measure can contribute to its larger goals.

For donors, they will know exactly what they're purchasing with the money they give.

CASH FLOW AND P&L

When that's done then the cost and expense necessary to build them will be included in the cash flow forecast or profit and loss projection. After that the plan for business creates an estimate of donation received or the charges that others pay due to planning activity.

Many non-profits' cash flow statement as well as the Profit and Loss Statement is the same. If you suspect that you'll incur accruals that differ from the cash account, I would suggest that you go through Chapter 7 of Your Cash Flow forecast and Capital Spending Plan starting on page 158 "How to Write an Business Plan Paperback 13th Edition, or page 153 , 'How to Write the Business Plan in a Paperback 12th edition. Talk to the advice of a CPA for doubts regarding the best way to draft this part.

The overall forecast of contributions or revenues may be placed on top in the P&L or in the middle.

The goal is to create an easily understood forecast of the total cash coming into and the total amount of money that is going out.

Chapter 14: What Is A Nonprofit?

In the beginning, all you must understand is what a nonprofit is. It is a non-profit entity that has been established for more than simply making profits. The majority of nonprofits are founded with the intention of promoting one cause or issue according to the perspective of a person(s) certain viewpoint. Also the nonprofit makes use of the money it earns to accomplish their objectives rather than focusing the funds to pay shareholders of the business.

The term "non-profit" is used in all countries to ensure everyone is aware of what an organization is doing. For the legal and accounting aspects There is a distinction between a nonprofit as well as a for-profit company. Similar to the distinct differences between non-profit businesses and for-profit companies.

A lot of people think of nonprofit organizations as a charity organizations. Although this may be valid to some extent.

There are many different nonprofit industry sectors. The term "non-profit" generally refers to one that serves members or is a community severing organisation. It is founded in order to have an impact on the members they serve or within their community.

Members-serving organisations are established for the purpose of serving the needs of a specific group of individuals. These include banks, sports clubs and retired serviceman's groups. They usually charge fee for memberships that help cover all the expenses members of the organisation.

The community-based organizations are in place to assist those in their communities or are even established to impact the world. They typically provide human services programs which include services like medical treatment to those who are unable to afford it. They also provide other services.

It is important to note that the purpose of a non-profit is in order to have an impact, instead of to earn money. The money that is deposited into the non-profit is utilized for the purpose of supporting the organisation. The money can be derived from membership dues or contributions to the nonprofit.

If you are considering starting your own business it is important to choose which nonprofits would like to establish. Most organizations are community-based non-profits which are set up in order to assist the people within their vicinity (obviously).

Let this not stop your progress, however, if you're planning to create an association that is staffed by members begin one. However, be sure to follow all guidelines set for the start of one. There could be a distinction in the requirements in a community service non-profit and a member-serving one.

Chapter 15: Research

One of the first things you must do prior to beginning your nonprofit organization is conduct your own study. What are the people you're trying to aid? What's your goal? Are you looking to become an organization that serves the community or would you like to become a member-serving group? The most important thing to consider is that a non-profit is still a company just like other company. The goals you set must be feasible and achievable. It is similar to creating a business for profit. You must have objectives that you can remember and achieve in the manner that was previously mentioned. When you are first beginning on your journey you should pretend you are already in charge of the organization and you are making decisions on behalf of an actual business. This allows you to determine if the choices you take are worthwhile taking and will actually have an effect or whether they could cause harm to your organization. Make a list of your objectives and see how you could write out your pros and cons are to setting up the non-profit.

This is a bit the same as writing your own business plan, only you're writing down the objectives you'd like to achieve as well as putting your ideas on paper so that you could really look at.

Here are some of the questions to consider when you are doing your homework.

Do you think there is a need for such an organization?

Does another company already in the process of doing exactly what I would like to achieve?

Do my objectives have a chance of being met?

What do I require to get in order to begin this business?

How fast will this company increase its size?

The best way to go about this is to take a seat and create your purpose declaration. What do you want to accomplish? The mission statement must describe the goals you're seeking to achieve. In essence, your mission statement must provide the answer to this big issue.

The reason this organisation exists?

This is an arduous one. If you are able to answer it the right way, you're on the way to setting the foundation of your own non-profit organization. If you are able to identify that other nonprofits who have already met these requirements Perhaps you could look into joining their work. The idea doesn't have to be a completely innovative idea; instead, you may take an idea which was already in motion and add your own spin to the idea. If, for instance, you're looking to aid children, look for something which isn't being used for helping the kids.

When you write your mission statements, make sure to try and incorporate values that define how your organization operates, its primary advantages and offerings to clients and how you'd like other people to perceive your organization and the various groups of customers that will be benefited by the services. This should be stated in order to ensure that people know your company's mission is, and that those who are working alongside you. They will know how to assist you in sticking to the mission you have set. It is crucial since you will adhere to the statement of your mission. The mission statement will come become the primary thing which your company is based upon. This will be what you do to make an impact.

The mission statement you write doesn't need to need to be a specific length must be. It could range between a couple of sentences and many pages. Be sure to ensure that you're concise and clear regarding what you'd like to convey. Do not leave room for any uncertainty. If there's a section that even you aren't sure over, then revise your mission declaration. Test your mission statement in the presence of different people to find out what they think about any aspect of it. The best approach is to make use of simple words to ensure it is simple to comprehend by everyone.

The other aspect of your investigation process is to figure out the type of non-profit you'd like to create. Are you looking for the organization to consist of you along with a handful of people? It's an idea to start the self-help groups in the community you live in. The type of non-profit is known as an informal non-profit. Its outreach is limited, but it still has an impact for those in desperate need. In the event that you start a tiny self-help organization, there's the chance that you're likely to grow larger than a single small self-help organization. If you and other volunteers from a non-profit organization want to start one, you could create multiple self-help groups across various areas within the area you live in so that people who can't get to as far are in a position to join the group in the event that they truly would like to.

Do you think your organization should be able to carry on after you've left? If this is the case then it's time to think about insuring your organization. When you do this it is ensuring it is registered as an entity that is legally distinct. This will ensure that it can remain that way. The nonprofit will be a separate entity and have its own assets and the bank accounts it owns and can even shield your personal assets from being held accountable. Be aware that when you form your non-profit it may require you to form a board directors.

A board of directors an organization of individuals that oversees the operations of your company and assist to make the right decision-making. Board of Directors are something like an advisory board. Instead of taking any decision independently it is possible to have the benefit of a team of experts that you can go to get their input. In certain organizations that have a board of directors, it is the director who is the one who makes all final decision. In the event that an individual is no longer competent to be employed by the company then the director's board would be the last panel to decide whether that employee is eligible to stay in the organization or likely to be dismissed.

Just like everything else that is tax-exempt, it will also have taxes. Speak with a tax professional or the IRS for advice on whether your nonprofit can be tax exempt or whether it is eligible to receive tax deductions. These two statuses determine the character of the organization along with the types of offerings being offered. If you are a business that relies on donations, it is possible to have chances that you'll be eligible for tax-deductible donations for these.

The two other things should be considered are your company in need of financial sponsors? Also, do you require legal counsel? A fiscal sponsor can to get started by assisting the organization because it doesn't have the resources needed to cover the initial expenses and costs that are associated when you start a non-profit organization. They will not only assist in the cost and expenses that come with starting your business and will also aid you in learning the techniques necessary to run the financial aspects of your non-profit. In the end, a sponsor is an established non-profit company that will assist you to become more successful in operating as a non-profit. It is also known as networking and the likelihood that you and the other organization work together is likely to happen.

Don't take this company for granted, and look to the organization for all your needs. Make your own mistakes to avoid the mistakes you make and then learn from their mistakes. If you're not sure if your mistake will harm your company You should talk to your fiscal manager to find out what they think and also consult the Board of Directors.

Once you've finished all that work and you'll want to ensure that it is protected as well as you. A lawyer for non-profits will assist protect all effort you've put into establishing your non-profit. Lawyers can assist to keep your organization from becoming an for-profit entity in addition to ensuring you fill all forms correctly for IRS on tax exemptions as well as tax deductions. An attorney will also be in a position to assist with opening the company's bank account, as well as obtaining insurance for employees that employ you, as well as how to ensure that you're complying with regulations of both the state and federal levels.

The costs related to the creation of the organization must be repaid. You can be sure that the local or state government might have a fee associated in keeping your non-profit operational. That is when hiring a professional lawyer as well as an accountant are helpful. Lawyers will inform to you about these charges and inform you of how much money will go toward; whereas an accountant can assist you in ensuring that charges are paid on time for your company to remain open.

The accountant is also helpful in ensuring that you maintain your non-profit's bank account within the regulations that are mandatory by law. The receipts for all transactions must be recorded for the income and expense. They will be useful for the purposes of filing tax returns for your non-profit organization.

Chapter 16: Fundraising

It's time to start your non-profit you have started your nonprofit! After all the study, you have finally got the mission statement nailed down as well as the people you want to join your organization and a fiscal manager who can guide you on how to manage your money and will assist to pay some of the initial costs. Additionally, you've submitted all of your paperwork to the IRS after submitting them to your lawyer. You've also made sure they're within the guidelines needed for a nonprofit. As of now it is likely that you have an executive board that helps to ensure that you do not make business-related decisions that may lead to your company shut down. All seems fine up until the point of. However, how do you planning to raise funds to continue running your non-profit?

The fundraising aspect is a factor. The first step is to have to determine what kind of fundraising you'd like to have. Another option is an fundraising event. The event can only be pulled off when you have an experienced staff is reliable so that it is possible to delegate work to specific members who will get the job completed. Events are an excellent method to get your financial sponsors on board and are a fantastic method of getting more people aware of the organization you run.

The event fundraiser is about obtaining donations of items that you'll auction off. You also need supporters to assist with entertainment, food drinks, the staff of the event as well as the location, publicity and invitations and on. These are only a small part of ensuring you're having an event that is successful. When you're planning your event, you're keeping your objectives in mind just like you did when looking for ways to begin your business.

If it's your first time hosting an event, make the event smaller to ensure that you will be able to observe how the event is going before deciding to create an event people will enjoy. However, when you start by having a smaller gathering test out new concepts you can come up with in order to attract donors, or find out what guests appreciate as well as dislike. Try to experiment with different ideas in a smaller crowd rather then to make a decision that could result in a significant amount of cash ultimately.

Another option is to organize various small-scale events throughout the year, which are put up in advance, so that guests are aware of the exact details. A lot of attendees return due to their belief in the values of the organization and wish to show their support by some manner, which is why they show up to events hosted by the organization.

One of the most important things is important to bear at the forefront when planning any fundraising event is the timeframe of the occasion. Do not put off your planning until the at the last minute, or else your event won't succeed as well as you'd like to make it. If you've decided on the theme of your event be sure there aren't any shady decoration that doesn't have anything to relate to the theme you've chosen. Be professional or perhaps even basic. Make sure you don't create a negative impression about your business or it may be difficult to come back.

If you don't have an extensive staff is able to delegate work to or hire an employee, consider an event fundraising event. This is a great option for groups with membership or congregations of churches. Think about the kinds of fundraising which schools organize, but using different items.

A good option is Auntie Anne's pretzels. A lot of people love Auntie Anne's and you could organize a fundraising event like this over a period of time so you're able to get more orders than you think possible. Don't restrict it to your area. Invite your participants to extend their reach to acquaintances, families, colleagues as well as anyone else willing to assist in making the event a hit. Another way you could make contact with people in the community is to put the location of a stand outside an area supermarket. This allows individuals to register who are willing to "donate" to your cause. When you do this be sure to let your patrons know they will see you at a certain date and in a certain time, in order to take their donations.

If you don't want to cook it is possible to also hold your own fundraiser with candles, or other items. Be sure to select something that will be a popular item for people to contribute money towards. The best thing to do is ensure that the item is something people can buy all throughout the year and could be a good item to offer as a present. A lot of people utilize fundraising events to buy gifts for birthdays, anniversaries and other holidays, as well as supporting an organization that is charitable or non-profit.

Be sure that whatever you choose to hold fundraising for is not too big and good-quality and also capable of being affordable.

There will be expenses associated to any fundraising event, such as transporting the goods to the place of the event and making payments to the business where the products are made however, the cost to cover these costs will not be from your pocket The company will cooperate together with you, and the costs will be included in the pricing. All you should be certain of is that you receive enough items for your price to be reduced by the cost of shipping and handling. All of us have financial problems. Remember, do you like spending the amount of money you did for that item? If not, why would you let someone else handle the work?

Like everything else that is legal, there are guidelines to fundraising for nonprofit organizations. If you don't adhere to these guidelines, you could be in danger of your company could face fines and you may lose your statutorily recognized status as a non-profit organization or be closed.

The first thing that you must complete is filling out the Unified Registration Statement (URS). The URS form will help gather all the information necessary for all nonprofits that conduct fundraising activities within their areas of responsibility. If your state is a member of the URS it is able to be utilized to register your organization. Your non-profit organization will be legally liable to registration requirements applicable to any state you're engaging in any fundraising activities. A few states have separate form that must be filled out. they require you to complete.

The states which do not use the URS include: Florida, Oklahoma, and Colorado. If you reside in these states you'll have to fill in the appropriate state forms. It is possible in the states mentioned above that you'll have to pay an appropriate check to cover any fee for registration, while filling in the correct forms before mail them back to the agency that administers them. In other states, however, everyone utilizes the URS and, if not, they will not require any forms to be completed. However, ensure that you ask your local as well as government officials to inform you whether they have paperwork that needs to be completed. Don't assume there's no cost or forms to fill in since you are in a state which is not a member of the URS. By doing so you could put your business at risk of closing down.

Like everything else, there are rules you have to follow. If you are hosting a fundraiser it is not advisable to employ a company to manage your event on your behalf because they will keep part of the funds so that they can pay everything they have to incur for running the occasion. This is the percentage of proceeds that go to the business could range from 90 to 100%, but only 10 percent of the money that is actually collected through the event will be donated towards your causes.

What would you think when you made a donation funds to an organization you were adamant about and then discover just a fraction of the money you give is being donated to this charity? If you would not inform your friends about everything what's the reason?

The whole point of raising money is to channel funds to the cause you want to support and not spend it on activities that divert funds from the goal. The entire purpose behind starting your non-profit organization was to expose your cause into a different perspective and to change the world to benefit your cause. That doesn't mean that you need to spend a lot of money or make it appear like they're from a discount department store, however it does not mean you need to spend an enormous amount of money for things which are essential.

In essence, you should keep track of your expenditure because at close of the year you will need to prove where the funds went to. If you are filing taxes, do it in order to preserve any tax relief or exemption the organization received through the IRS. Each donation that is made to the nonprofit is to be tracked in order to verify that you do not claim the status of a nonprofit even though you're not a non-profit corporation.

Then there's the local business that is around your non-profit that might have the capacity to give to your nonprofit. Many businesses have a budget on this side for charity giving. Businesses can contribute more than others based on revenues, but they're constantly willing to assist if it's within the budget. Although they may not be able to financial aid, they all the time are willing to put flyers for any events might be happening at some point in the future.

www.ingramcontent.com/pod-product-compliance
Lightning Source LLC
Chambersburg PA
CBHW070556010526
44118CB00012B/1342